Sacred Cows Make the Best Barbecue

Sacred Cows Make the Best Barbecue

Supply Chain Management:
A Revolutionary 26-Week Action Plan

Chip Long
Dr. Gay Meyer

VISION+
PRESS

Seal Beach, California

ISBN 0-96611-551-1

Designed by:
   The ART of Communications
   Snow Harbor Graphics

Vision+ Press
P.O. Box 3417
Seal Beach, CA 90740

Printed in Canada

Acknowledgements

To the believers, supporters, critics, and practitioners who have attended our seminars over the years: You have all contributed to this book. The impetus to write *Sacred Cows Make the Best Barbecue* was a direct result of your thirst for knowledge. Without your belief, commitment, and enthusiasm, we wouldn't have attempted to harness that flood of ideas and put it between the pages of a book.

We must also give special thanks to the many clients who over the years have reconfirmed our belief in Supply Chain Management. It is through their efforts and the results they showed that we know the process described in this book positively works.

Finally, we are indebted to the editorial efforts of Ben Hughes and Arthur Levine. This book owes much to their thorough, rigorous, and thoughtful comments. Without Ben and Arthur's hard work, this book would still be an idea, not a reality.

Writing a book is a labor of love. Fortunately, we have a passion for Supply Chain Management. It is our belief that Supply Chain Management is simply not an option for your company. The only choices are *when* you make the commitment and *how fast* you implement it. Change is always difficult. But for those who do adopt Supply Chain Management, the rewards are infinite. We hope this book speeds you on your way.

Contents

Our Journey

The best salespeople are those who have a passion for the product they are selling. We caught our passion for Supply Chain Management from others. During the years of consulting and teaching, we have had the pleasure of participating in some truly amazing Supply Chain Management success stories. Harley-Davidson, Motorola, Honda, NCR, Gateway, Anheuser-Busch, Boeing, Whirlpool, Chrysler, Intel, Xerox, Sherwin Williams, to name just a few... all great companies, all passionate about finding radically new and better ways of dealing with their suppliers.

Our introduction to Supply Chain Management came in the early '80s, when offshore competition awoke this country to Just-In-Time concepts. Unfortunately, many did not take the time to understand and master the basics of JIT. Others struggled to adopt JIT, but fell short. Manufacturing is rife with "sacred cows" and they're hard to kill. But those who made the conversion would be the first to proclaim that the results more than justify the effort.

From those early days, our clients who implemented supplier report cards, quantitative supplier assessments, and supplier performance indexes achieved results that could not have been attained through traditional procurement practices. Today we are more convinced than ever that Supply Chain Management is the best way to manage the supplier-customer relationship.

In today's global economy, 40% to 80% of our manufacturing costs are spent on materials bought from a supplier. Supply Chain Management is not a quick fix; it's an indisputably superior way to work with suppliers. The recent fourth integrated Supply Chain

Performance Benchmarking Study performed by Pittiglio, Rabin, Todd, & McGrath (PRTM) shows that companies save between 3% and 7% of annual revenues with SCM. That's not small change.

We wish you the best of luck on your Supply Chain Management journey. By following the steps in this book, you too can become more successful in your relationships with your suppliers. Our most fervent hope is that this book helps you to become passionate about Supply Chain Management and that you'll start "selling" it, too.

Finally, never forget those famous words from Dr. Deming: "You don't have to do this, survival is not compulsory."

Let your journey begin!

Chip Long
Dr. Gay Meyer
Seal Beach, California
December, 1997

About This Book

" No firm is an island. Your customers depend on the excellence of your suppliers. "

Daniel Jones
Co-author of *The Machine that Changed the World*

North America manufacturers have finally woken up to the revelation that purchasing and Supply Chain Management are critically important components of the business strategy. In fact, they are so important in today's highly competitive global market that a company's success depends upon its ability to fully integrate purchasing and Supply Chain Management into its overall business strategy.

However, acknowledging the strategic importance of the supply chain is only half the battle. Accompanying it must come the recognition that the traditional way of doing business with suppliers needs radical revision, starting with the removal of some much-revered "sacred cows." For too many years, the purchasing world has held the following principles to be sacred...

- Three quotes... buy low
- Many suppliers for the same product
- Short-term supplier relationships
- Supplier not involved in design phase
- Purchase price variance (PPV) reporting
- Lack of trust between supplier and customer
- Pass-fail supplier audits

Historically, the supplier relationship in North America has been adversarial and based on the short-term view that purchase price is the most important consideration when dealing with suppliers. That's finally changing. Company executives are discovering that in an era of increasingly complex global competition, adversarial relationships often work against their company's best interests. They inhibit companies from getting at the root cause of defects in products and services.

Now is the time to light a fire under the people in your company and use it to barbecue those sacred cows. Supply Chain Management is one of the most focused and comprehensive processes to hit the procurement area in 20 years. Adopt it in your company, and you'll see measurable improvements in quality, delivery, costs, and most importantly, profits. For many companies, the savings are measured in the millions of dollars.

Join the Manufacturing Revolution

In the pages that follow, you'll learn how to take part in the Supply Chain Management revolution. In the immediate sense, you'll find out how to revolutionize the way your company works with its suppliers. In the larger sense, however, you'll be joining the rebirth of North American manufacturing that began in the 1970s. That's when, overnight it seemed, the world's manufacturing superpower was revealed as a bloated, crippled giant. Whole industries were lost to nimble overseas competitors that could make things better *and* cheaper.

In the midst of those dark days, the seeds of renewal were sown. Once-arrogant companies began a painful process of self-examination. For the first time they looked to foreign competitors for better ways of doing things. Gradually, lessons were learned, changes were made. The process is far from complete, but it's working. Humbler, but also smarter and leaner, North American companies are competing and winning again. By bringing Supply Chain Management into your company, you'll be keeping this manufacturing renaissance alive.

As you may have guessed, many of the techniques discussed in this book were first employed overseas, often in Japan. That does not mean you're expected to transform your company into a Japanese-style operation. We all know it can't be done, nor should it be. The methods of Supply Chain Management that you'll learn in this book are designed for North American companies. They encompass principles that you can easily learn and that your company can apply.

We also want to note that the rewards of Supply Chain Management aren't reserved for the giants. Almost any company willing to commit to the steps outlined in this book can reap the benefits. In fact, Supply Chain Management may be most helpful to "the other guys"—smaller, more entrepreneurial companies and subsidiaries with the willingness to try new ideas.

Sacred Cows (outmoded purchasing practices) vs. new Supply Chain Management techniques

Sacred Cows	SCM
Purchase based on price	Purchase based on total cost of ownership
Multiple suppliers, just in case	Single supplier based on supplier performance
P.O. to P.O. buying	Evergreen contracts
No supplier input in design phase	Supplier involved in pre-design and design phases
Purchase price variance	Cost reduction targets based on cost analysis
Customer-supplier relationship is distant, possibly adversarial	Customer-supplier relationship is integrated and mutually beneficial
Pass-fail supplier audits	Continuous improvement

Designed For Action: 13 Steps, 26 Weeks

In the process of getting rid of the sacred cows of purchasing, we're going to take the mystery out of Supply Chain Management. When we began this book, our intention was to produce an action plan for your company, laid out in concrete steps. We believe we've succeeded. We hope you'll find this book easy to read and a handy companion that you'll want to open again and again. And, we believe you'll find it useful, regardless of whether your company is just now considering Supply Chain Management or has already embarked on a program to rethink the way it does business with its suppliers.

We've also added a time component, indicating the week you should **begin** each step. The schedule is ambitious—a best-case scenario. However, from long experience we know an aggressive plan is what it takes to succeed. It's especially important to move speedily through setting up the Supply Chain Management system within your company. If you can get your internal systems in place and are ready to go out and perform tactical supply chain assessments on your suppliers (Step 9), you're in good shape. The fastest, most committed companies will keep to the schedule suggested. Others will take longer—up to seven months—to reach that point. After that, however, momentum will decrease rapidly. In our experience, companies that aren't performing their assessments within a year face a 50% chance that their SCM program will die on the drawing board. If you see your program ratcheting down the priority list, act quickly or it may die. Keep up the momentum!

Our Promise To You

This book stacks the deck in your favor. If you follow the prescriptions, you can make it happen. The actual work that's necessary will be done by people from middle management and below in the company hierarchy. However, the size of your victory will depend upon top management's commitment. If you can get the executive suite behind your program, you'll experience substantial improvements. How substantial? With an effective SCM program, your company can expect to:

- Reduce the price of procurement by 20-30%
- Reduce the price of non-conformance by 30-50%
- Reduce inventory levels by 30-90%
- Reduce your total product cycle time by 40-60%

Read this book. Learn the principles of Supply Chain Management. Find other committed people and form a team. Begin with manageable steps. You may find it difficult to barbecue your sacred cows and the going may be slow at times, but stick with the program. If you do, we promise that your company *will* reap significant rewards.

Committing to Supply Chain Management as a Strategic Business Function

" If you think you are going to be successful running your business in the next ten years the way you did in the last ten years, you're out of your mind. To succeed, we have to disturb the present. "

Roberto Goizueta,
Coca-Cola

Do you think *that setting out to change the traditional pattern of dealing with your suppliers is doomed before you even start? Think again. Few companies can match the Big Three auto makers when it comes to rigidity in dealing with suppliers. Yet Chrysler deliberately set out to totally rebuild its supplier relationship. To say that they succeeded is an understatement. From a traditional two-year bid process, Chrysler has moved to agreements with suppliers for the life of a car model. Detailed contracts have been replaced with oral agreements. Price terms are worked out with the supplier, instead of handed down by fiat. Chrysler engineers have loosened their hold on design and have begun to involve suppliers to an unprecedented degree. In the process, the total number of suppliers has shrunk from 2,500 to 1,140. What's the point? As detailed in an article by Jeffrey Dyer in the July-August* Harvard Business Review, *the point is profits:*

"The results have been astounding. The time Chrysler needs to develop a new vehicle is approaching 160 weeks, down from an average of 234 weeks during the 1980s. The cost of developing a new vehicle has plunged an estimated 20% to 40% during the last decade to less than $1 billion for the Cirrus/Stratus,

*introduced this year. And, at the same time, Chrysler has managed to produce
one customer hit after another—including the Neon, the Dodge Ram truck, the
Cirrus/Stratus, and the new minivan (sold as the Town & Country, Dodge
Caravan, and Plymouth Voyager). As a result, Chrysler's profit per vehicle has
jumped from an average of $250 in the 1980s to a record (for all U.S. automak-
ers) of $2,110 in 1994."*

*Isn't that enough of a reason for your company to begin the Supply Chain
Management journey?*

Beginning the Journey

For the purposes of this book, commitment to Supply Chain
Management is the starting point: Step 1, Week 1. Gaining that
commitment, however, may take you weeks or months, depending upon your industry, your company's top management, and
your position in the company. To gain that support, you'll need to make
the case for SCM. Most of this chapter will discuss why radically
changing the way you deal with your suppliers could be the most
important business move you ever make. We'll show why the most successful companies in the biggest, fastest growing industries have
adopted SCM. And we'll discuss a plan for consolidating support in
your company once you've gained a toehold. It's an exciting journey,
so let's begin!

Why Change?

Before we examine Supply Chain Management, we have to look at the
traditional relationship between purchaser and supplier. In the most
stripped-down, classical definition, your supplier is a company from
which you elect to purchase a product or service, usually on the basis

of price. For North American manufacturers, the time-honored scenario has been to pit suppliers against each other in cutthroat competitive bidding, with the lowest price winning the contract. A supplier's record on "intangibles," such as quality and timeliness, has counted for little against the almighty price.

The relationship between purchaser and supplier, it has usually been assumed, is adversarial. With an agreement centered on price, the stage is set for both parties to attempt to get the better end of the deal. Many of us are all too familiar with suppliers who underbid to win a contract, then cut corners in a scramble to realize a profit. On the opposite side of the table are purchasers who demand expensive changes and extras, all within the contracted price. Then, at the end of the contracted period, the supplier is back at the starting line. Regardless of track record or investments in plant and equipment on behalf of the customer, the supplier must again compete for the contract. Is it any wonder that supplier and purchaser often view each other with suspicion and bad feelings?

Towards a New Partnership

At its very heart, Supply Chain Management restructures this classic, but fundamentally flawed, relationship. In its place, you'll create a **partnership**. Like any real partnership, it's built on trust, mutual benefit, responsibility, longevity and fairness. As you'll discover, lowering the barriers and creating a partnership opens the door for surprising, even radical, changes to take place. The hunt for an ever-lower price recedes into the background as the emphasis shifts to the best **value.**

In addition, supplier relationships begin to extend for the life of a product, rather than the life of a contract. Depending upon the industry you're in, representatives from your suppliers may become valued members of your development team. And you'll guarantee that your supplier will make a profit. Of course, it's not all one-sided. You'll be looking for much in exchange. But they'll be goals that you and your suppliers will work on together, and from which you both stand to gain.

What Is Supply Chain Management?

In the simplest terms, Supply Chain Management is the process of establishing performance criteria for each of your suppliers, then auditing on a regular basis to make sure the criteria are met. However, SCM begins by taking a look at your whole manufacturing process, including your supplier base. You'll have to determine what your real requirements are, decide what constitutes acceptable performance by a supplier, and establish your true cost of procurement. It means reevaluating your internal processes, possibly even restructuring departments and scrapping sacred rituals that may have been observed since long before you arrived at the company.

Implementing Supply Chain Management will not be easy. However, there is one all-encompassing reason to embark on this journey: Simply put, SCM will make your company more competitive, now and in the future.

What It Costs to Build a Product

In the remainder of this chapter, we'll look at the real impact of suppliers on your company, the benefits of Supply Chain Management, and the kinds of barriers you'll encounter on the way to putting your program in place. Finally, we'll discuss specific methods for winning support for Supply Chain Management.

Many companies overlook the full impact of materials on the cost of making a product. When North American manufacturers have gone looking for places to save, labor has historically been the target. Saving on labor generally allows two options: automate or manufacture out of the country.

As illustrated in Figure 1-1, however, even in industries with highly paid labor forces, such as automotive and aerospace, rarely does labor exceed 15% of the cost of the product. Material costs, ranging from

40%-80%, constitute the lion's share of making a product. This ratio has not gone unnoticed. As the dust settles from the whirlwind of corporate downsizing that grabbed headlines in the early and mid-1990s, many companies are turning to purchasing as the next frontier of cost-cutting. Fortune 500 companies in many industries, including AT&T, Allied Signal, and Owens Corning, have begun vigorous campaigns to slash the amount they pay for everything from consulting services to paper clips. In other words, you won't be alone in looking to your supply chain for savings.

Beyond Price: How Suppliers Have an Impact on Your Company

We may find it convenient to think of supply mainly in terms of price, but suppliers have a much broader impact on your company. Only by recognizing the full extent of their role can we begin to forge new relationships. By learning to think beyond the "price-only" mentality, you'll begin to formulate new performance criteria for your suppliers. In fact, just by reviewing the following four topics you'll probably find yourself mentally categorizing individual suppliers.

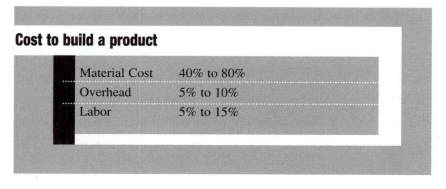

Cost to build a product

Material Cost	40% to 80%
Overhead	5% to 10%
Labor	5% to 15%

Figure 1-1. *Material costs can be quite significant.*

Costs: Your suppliers' impact in this area can be divided into direct and indirect costs. The easiest way to separate the two is by the maxim, "If you can measure it, it's direct." That is, if you can assign a specific dollar amount to a specific supplier, consider it a direct cost. For most companies, that's limited to the cost of materials and freight. Gray areas such as scrap, rework, and early and late delivery, on the other hand, fall under the indirect cost heading. Even though it may be very difficult to track an indirect cost like scrap back to a single supplier, you can learn to measure—and limit—your indirect cost totals.

Inventory investment: Suppliers can effect inventory investment in several ways. You may have to carry a relatively high inventory of your completed product because of the difficulty of "restarting" your supply chain to manufacture new lots. Or, one or two suppliers may have a much longer lead time than others, requiring you to carry substantial "safety stock" of their material or component. Supply Chain Management will enable you to reduce some of this inventory. How much depends upon your industry and your suppliers. Companies like Harley-Davidson that have established vigorous and effective Just-In-Time manufacturing programs have all but eliminated component inventories. If your company depends upon overseas suppliers, on the other hand, you may not be able to do away with extra stock.

Planning/scheduling: The amount of lead time you have to build into your schedules to accommodate your suppliers has a direct impact on your ability to serve your customers. But don't look just to your suppliers for the solution. This is an area where your supplier partnership can really pay off. The earlier you involve your suppliers in your plans, the better they can meet your schedules and the schedules of your customers.

Conformance to specifications: As with scheduling, don't lay all the blame for inability to meet spec on your suppliers. Before providing part specs to your supplier, you must have 100% agreement within your company on what those specs are and if they are within generally accepted industry standards. In a traditional product development cycle, organized by function, parts are often specified independent of feedback from the supplier, or even from the purchasing department. Too often, companies end up with unrealistic specifications and parts that simply cannot be produced within given tolerances on a consistent basis. The company gets stuck with a high rate of scrap or rework. Even more damaging, this extra burden soon becomes "invisible" and is considered just part of the cost of doing business.

Why Your Company Needs SCM

In the introduction to this book, we spelled out some ambitious percentage improvements your company can achieve with Supply Chain Management. In reality, the increasingly competitive global economy makes improvements like these a necessity—now. Don't file them away as pie-in-the-sky goals to be achieved at some unspecified date in the far-off future.

If you have any reluctance about embarking on a program to completely revamp your relationship with your suppliers, just remind yourself that each goal of Supply Chain Management is one that your competitors are striving for, too. Continuous improvement, cost savings, reduced inventory, shortened cycle time, and financial leverage and flexibility: these aren't vague mission statements, these are simply the cost of competing today. The good news is that with Supply Chain Management, goals like those enumerated in the introduction are well within your grasp. If a company as massive and tradition-bound as Chrysler can radically revamp its relationship with its suppliers, then your company can, too.

Why SCM Benefits Your Suppliers, Too

When they first get wind of it, don't be surprised if your suppliers view your Supply Chain Management program with suspicion. Given the exploitative nature of the traditional customer-supplier relationship, it's only human nature that they'll expect the worst. You may find that a supplier seizes on a single component of SCM, such as supplier report cards, fearing that you'll use them to force concessions. Others may recall horror tales about early implementation of Just-In-Time programs in this country. At that time, some auto manufacturers used their purchasing clout to impose crippling demands on suppliers. The cost of doing business with these major buyers included orders to move plants, begin daily, even hourly, deliveries, and achieve zero defects—ASAP!

In short, the supplier community tends to be wary of big changes in the traditional way of doing business—even if the old ways contain plenty of problems, too. It's the old adage about being happier with the devil you know than the devil you don't know.

In fact, your suppliers' fears won't be entirely unfounded. In the course of implementing your SCM program, you'll be taking a close look at your supply requirements and at all your suppliers. Reducing your supply base is one of the primary goals of Supply Chain Management. As noted in the excerpt at the beginning of this chapter, Chrysler cut its suppliers to less than half when it reformed its supply base.

However, the benefits of Supply Chain Management to suppliers are many, and they're well documented. It will be important that you understand the full implications of a SCM program before you involve your suppliers. Later sections of the book provide techniques for bringing your suppliers on board and making them committed "converts." And remember, SCM is a learning process both for you and for your suppliers. One maxim which we fully believe is that superior suppliers are developed, not found.

Some of the specific benefits your suppliers can anticipate from Supply Chain Management include:

- A committed, long-term relationship with your company
- Increased business with your company

- Designation as the supplier of choice for new products
- Early involvement in new product design
- Clear communication of materials requirements
- Assistance from your company in meeting those requirements
- Improved terms of payment

The Supplier-Customer Synergy

Finally, the partnership between you and your suppliers will create a powerful synergy. You can expect results that neither party could achieve on its own. Shared resources, shared responsibility, and trust are potent forces in any union. In your supplier partnership, they can help both parties achieve ongoing cost reductions, continuous quality improvement, reduced product cycle times, better use of technology, and more powerful competitive strategies. The phrase "win-win" gets a little overused these days, but when discussing a successful Supply Chain Management program, it's completely appropriate.

Gaining Support

Even with suppliers who embrace your SCM initiative, you'll have your work cut out for you putting your program in place. Just remember: preparation is half the battle. Anticipate the obstacles, and you'll be better ready to counter them. They'll range from potential program killers, such as indifference or outright hostility from upper management, to problems springing mainly from a misunderstanding of what SCM is all about and how it works.

When you do encounter resistance to Supply Chain Management (and you will!), do not simply throw up your hands. Instead, identify the specific source of resistance, whether it's a person, a procedure, or a matter of company organization. Speak to the person or the people involved. Listen, and listen well, to their concerns. Don't try to address every issue on the spot. Offer to get back to them. Then carefully lay out how SCM works in the area about which they're concerned. Enlist allies. As you'll discover in Step 2, preaching the "gospel" of SCM will be one of the team's most important tasks. Recruit team members who can help spread the word. Most obstacles can be overcome with persistence and education. And remember, SCM produces measurable benefits. All you need is the chance; the proof will arrive on its own.

Tapping Outside Assistance

One important way to get your program under way is to enlist the support of an outside resource. For some reason, people need to hear the truth from someone outside their company—even when they already know it's the truth. It's something we've seen confirmed again and

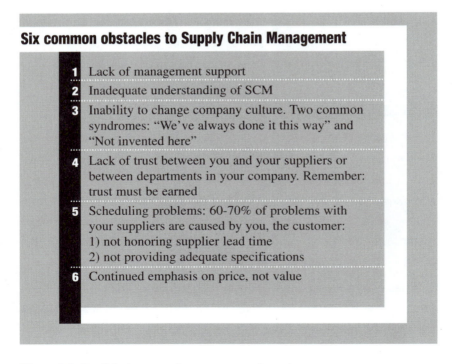

Six common obstacles to Supply Chain Management

1 Lack of management support

2 Inadequate understanding of SCM

3 Inability to change company culture. Two common syndromes: "We've always done it this way" and "Not invented here"

4 Lack of trust between you and your suppliers or between departments in your company. Remember: trust must be earned

5 Scheduling problems: 60-70% of problems with your suppliers are caused by you, the customer: 1) not honoring supplier lead time 2) not providing adequate specifications

6 Continued emphasis on price, not value

Figure 1-2. *Roadblocks you and your team may face.*

again, both while working for organizations in a variety of industries and in 15 years of consulting. Perhaps people need to validate their own instincts. Maybe they mistrust the motives of the people with whom they work. Oliver Goldsmith, the 18th-century British poet and novelist, put it most succinctly: "People seldom improve when they have no model but themselves to copy." For whatever reason, an outside resource can neutralize suspicion and help give SCM a free and fair hearing.

Our business is consulting and educating, as you may know. You're forgiven, therefore, for thinking that we're putting in a plug for ourselves when we suggest bringing in someone from outside the company. However, your outside resource doesn't necessarily have to be a paid consultant. It can be a customer or supplier who has already become an expert at Supply Chain Management. Chrysler had a supplier so successful at incorporating the practices of lean manufacturing that it enlisted the supplier's people to mentor Chrysler employees. Your outside resource can even be a new employee who comes from a company with a successful SCM program. Introduce that person as a

Supply Chain Management education

Who should attend	Length of presentation
Management	3 to 4 hours
Buyers, QC, Design Engineers, Manufacturing Engineers, Materials, and Shop Floor Supervisors not on the SCM team.	$1/2$ to 1 day
SCM Team	1 to 2 days

Figure 1-3. *Present your SCM case in educational programs.*

"change agent" and have him or her serve as your head evangelist. Be sure to act quickly, though. It will only take a few months before your evangelist's fresh ideas have been papered over by your company's entrenched culture.

We will make one plug for our own trade: The role for which we do strongly recommend a qualified SCM consultant is to present a company-wide educational program. Here's where having someone who can speak from long experience, field any question, and cite numerous examples of SCM success is invaluable. In other words, this is where you take your carefully prepared case for SCM and turn it over to Perry Mason to present to the jury. Figure 1-3 briefly outlines who should attend an SCM educational program and for how long.

Step 1 EXERCISE
Selling Supply Chain Management

One sure killer of any innovative strategy is resistance within the company. Don't fall into the trap, however, of confusing normal caution with real opposition. Even in innovative companies, people need to be persuaded. In fact, your ability to win support for Supply Chain Management will be the first sign of the strength of your program. One of the best ways to counter resistance is to analyze it, isolate it, understand it, and devise a strategy for overcoming it. When you do, you'll often find that what you perceived as general resistance boils down to some initial hesitancy and a few loud voices.

In the chart on the next page, identify the most serious areas of resistance and record the nature and strength of the objection. Then, jot down a line of counterattack. Don't agonize over this exercise. Its purpose is to help you generate some action. Remember, once you win over one or two opponents, the others will begin to fall into line as you build a consensus. We've filled in the first one as an example.

Overcome SCM resistance at your company

	Area/Department	Objection	Resistance*
1	Purchasing	Suppliers can't be trusted	B
	Strategy: Win agreement from Gil Jones for 1-year trial		
2			
	Strategy:		
3			
	Strategy:		
4			
	Strategy:		
5			
	Strategy:		

*A=strong, B=moderate, C=low

Figure 1-4. *Specify strategies to break through resistance.*

Putting the Team Together

" None of us is as smart as all of us. *"*

Anonymous

As you might expect, *you can run into formidable obstacles when forming teams that cross departmental boundaries. For example, when we helped to implement a Supply Chain Management program at the medical device division of a major healthcare company, the "core four" was to consist of representatives from design engineering, manufacturing engineering, materials purchasing, and quality. However, things got off to a bad start immediately because the design engineers refused to participate. "We're working on the next generation of products and haven't got time for this," was the excuse.*

The other team members carried on without them, and participated with great enthusiasm. It soon became evident, however, that the director of manufacturing engineering, who was not on the team, wanted nothing to do with SCM. He would overrule any action his engineers wanted to take on behalf of the team. "My staff takes direction from me, not the team," was his comment.

The fact that the company's culture had always encouraged "Lone Ranger" types who seized initiative, took strong ownership of projects, and got the job done gave him credibility. We had strong support from the vice president of operations, but he believed in consensus management and thought the director of ME would eventually come around.

In the end, despite the obstacle, Supply Chain Management saved the company $2 million the first year. The director of ME voluntarily resigned shortly thereafter. Company-wide support for SCM shot up. The message: If you can just get to that first set of measurable results, you can win over a lot of skeptics.

Once your company makes the commitment to establish Supply Chain Management, the next step will be to build the internal supply chain team. These are the people who will be responsible for designing and implementing the program and preaching the SCM gospel. Since the concepts and ways of conducting business will differ radically from your company's established modes, preaching will be a major focus of the team.

Don't underestimate the importance of your SCM missionary work. We have yet to encounter a company in which somebody didn't have to be sold on the idea of SCM, whether it was middle management, hourly employees, the suppliers, or the executives. Typically the sales pitch is directed to all of the above and it's not a one-time effort. You'll be proposing a re-alignment of core business practices. The team will need to wage an ongoing public relations campaign throughout the company. But it's not all smoke and mirrors; the selling points for Supply Chain Management will be based on tangible measurements. Skeptical co-workers will buy into SCM when they see bottom-line evidence of its value.

Faced with these formidable tasks, it will be essential to pull together the right people for the team. Good interpersonal skills and the ability to forge effective relationships will be crucial. The SCM team will serve as a model. It will set the tone for the program both within the company and in outside alliances with suppliers. You will need to identify non-adversarial people who can work together constructively on common goals.

In some cases, it will be a challenge to get anyone interested in participating on the SCM team. Who among us in this downsized era isn't already overwhelmed by our day-to-day duties? How can we ask anyone to add this responsibility to an overloaded schedule? There is one time-tested place to start. The old adage, "If you want to get something done, ask the busiest person" still holds true. Regardless of their heavy workload, the most committed people are the most likely to be enticed by the opportunity to effect real change. They may also have the foresight to understand that SCM will ultimately make their lives easier. However, if people don't rush to join your team, there is the standard fall-back tactic: Have senior management tell targeted staff to "volunteer."

Since SCM represents a wholesale culture change, it will be important to incorporate team members from throughout the company. Not only will you want the input and expertise of many departments, change will be embraced more readily when a broad representation of the company takes ownership of the process. Your goal, then, will be to establish a cross-functional team whose influence will reach far and wide.

Who Should Be on the Team?

The "core four"

An effective SCM team (or almost any productive team, for that matter) will ideally have four to seven members. With fewer than four participants, the team will not be getting input or representation from some key departments. Also, a small team and its mission will not be perceived as important within the company. With more than ten members, meetings can become unwieldy and unfocused and progress can be restricted.

Seek senior employees for your team. By "senior," we're not referring to a person's title or status within the company. Nor are we suggesting you choose team members according to their age. It is senior experience which will most benefit your team. By recruiting the people within your company who have the most longevity in their departments, you'll be helping to stack the deck in your favor. SCM team members must be flexible and welcome change. Senior employees will bring the most to the table: knowledge, resources, influence, and insight. They can offer a long view of where your company has been in order to prepare it for the Supply Chain Management journey ahead. Avoid long-time employees, however, who are resistant to change and stuck in their ways.

While the composition of the team will vary according to the nature of the industry, effective SCM teams generally look remarkably similar. As Figure 2-1 illustrates, the first four departments to tap for participants will be purchasing, quality, manufacturing, and engineering. We refer to these critical departments as the "core four." Typically, purchasing and quality are the departments most ready to adopt SCM.

Purchasing:

It's unusual for all of the "core four" departments to jump on board at

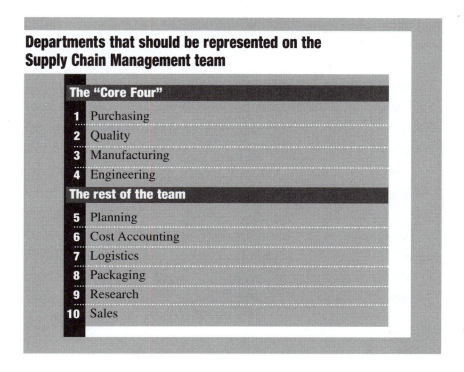

Figure 2-1. *The Supply Chain team.*

the outset. Be prepared for resistance, even from these standard-bearers of the supply chain. Purchasing agents are a company's direct link in the supply chain. However, they may be so entrenched in the traditional ways of doing business that they will be unable to recognize the long-term benefits of SCM. More than any other department, the people in purchasing are driven by price. For them, the lure of a great deal is powerful. It can take purchasing longer to learn the mantra of "value, value, value" when all they've ever known is "price, price, price." Worse, in some situations, purchasing employees receive under-the-table perks. The beneficiaries won't want to see the gravy train end.

The SCM team will have the responsibility for ensuring that products meet your "new" 100%-agreed-upon engineering specifications. Purchasing's SCM role will be to certify that the specifications from engineering can be produced by the supplier. In many instances, engineering develops a specification with such demanding tolerances, no supplier can realistically meet the specifications. The result is waivers in the receiving inspection area. It also sends the message that quality is a moving target based on the need to meet monthly production and shipping quotas. If a supplier says that your tolerances cannot be met, purchasing must find a new supplier or have engineering change the specifications. (See Step 8.)

The SCM purchasing representative must also ensure that the supplier is making a fair profit. In a traditional purchasing negotiation, the supplier sacrifices profit margin to satisfy a price point. Purchasing and the supplier cast a wary eye at each other. Seldom do both feel the final deal is satisfactory. Reductions in the supplier's prices are more likely to be win/win scenarios, however, using the Supply Chain Management approach. In this arrangement, the two sides work together to improve the process and both reap the benefits of price reductions.

Quality:

The quality department can be your strongest ally. However, the quality staff may be concerned about what will happen to their department when inspection and testing have been significantly reduced—or eliminated—after your suppliers have radically improved their quality performance. This is a legitimate issue that can impede SCM acceptance. There are some strategies you may want to consider. Some companies place post-SCM QC staff as "consultants" in suppliers' facilities for process capability (improvement) studies. The quality control staff can also be used to pre-qualify new suppliers by conducting on-site assessments at candidates' facilities. (See Step 6.)

The quality control representative on your SCM team will need to ensure that your suppliers' products can be inspected and tested based on the new specifications you produce. QC will also be valuable collecting receiving data (deviations, scrap, rework) for rating suppliers' quality.

Manufacturing:

Members of your manufacturing department might not initially understand their role on the SCM team and may attempt to back away from involvement. But the department's participation on the SCM team is critical. Acting as the internal customer, manufacturing makes sure that products received from the supplier produce the expected yields in your manufacturing and assembly process. The department will also collect shop floor data that will be used to rate your suppliers' quality performance.

Engineering:

As in the story at the beginning of the section, don't be surprised if your engineers say they're too busy developing a new product line to help out your SCM team. But the engineering department has a key SCM role to play. Your engineers will make sure that timely changes are made to the drawings and specifications upon which your suppliers and SCM team agrees. In addition, engineers must become knowledgeable about your suppliers' processes and capabilities in order to guarantee that cost targets and quality yields can be met.

However, expect some apprehension among engineers from your company when they are asked to allow one of their designs to be tweaked by a supplier's engineer. Some engineers are known to subscribe to the "I invented it here" syndrome. Your engineers may also be reluctant to loosen design tolerances, as already noted. Engineers who have been cloistered for too long can be a problem. They may have little understanding about your company's manufacturing processes, let alone the capabilities of your suppliers and the industry at large. When a company reaches consensus on all of these issues and demonstrates SCM success, the engineering department, along with manufacturing, purchasing, and quality—the "core four"—will join the team.

The Rest of the Team

Your company's unique needs will determine which department members join and the extent of their participation

It might be tempting to include the CEO on the Supply Chain Management team. There is no better example of corporate commitment or access to power. But, realistically, will he or she be able to attend all the planning meetings? Whether it's the CEO or some other high-ranking official, however, it will be important to have an executive-level champion of the SCM cause. Teams will need someone to articulate their message or occasionally run interference. One way to involve the CEO or other executives without overburdening them is to establish an "SCM executive committee." These influential people can be kept apprised of developments at periodic meetings while the SCM team lays the groundwork and does the hands-on work.

Beyond the "core four," representatives from the departments listed in Figure 2-1 may or may not serve as permanent members on your team. Team leaders will want to determine an individual's overall value to the process before assigning a role. Depending on the type of business, some companies might want to involve certain team members on an as-needed basis. For instance, a member from **logistics** might be helpful when there are special transportation considerations for a particular supply, such as arranging air-conditioned vehicles. On the other hand, when a company works towards Just-In-Time supply, a full-time logistics team member can help calculate inventory cost savings against increased transportation costs.

Here are two scenarios in which a person from **packaging** could sit on the SCM team: 1) The products under discussion require protective packaging to prevent mishandling or damage in transit; or, 2) The supplies require packaging that will appeal to consumers and/or customers. The **research** department is typically represented on the team when new products are being developed. Replacing the engineering slot in some companies, research departments often bring in initial suppliers for prototyping. Again, the decision to include someone on the team from the research, packaging, **planning**, or **cost accounting** departments, either as permanent members or as-needed, will be driven by the nature of the company's industry and its unique needs.

It's no mistake that **sales** is listed last on the list. Quality improvement has not traditionally been a major concern of most salespeople. Since ISO 9000, however, people from sales are jumping on the bandwagon. They understand that quality and other SCM principles offer them new ways to package their messages and get their feet in the door.

MIS is a possible addition to the list of potential SCM team members since their ability to track information, produce reports, and modify recordkeeping systems can be crucial to the supply chain process. But like others on the list, they probably will best serve the team on an as-needed basis.

What Are the Team's Responsibilities?
It's important to establish common goals and objectives

1. **Sell the SCM program to the company**

2. **Sell the SCM program to suppliers**

3. Develop supplier selection criteria

4. Develop rating system/report card

5. Develop survey/report card

6. Administer the Supply Chain Management program

In order to work effectively, you'll want to make sure your members have a clear understanding of the SCM team's mission. Team members need to be on the same page at the program's inception and throughout its early stages. Here's more about each goal:

1. Sell the SCM program to the company

A successful SCM team builds bridges among departments. The program will simply not work if the team works in isolation. The team will develop the SCM infrastructure but the company will carry out the program.

The initial objective will be to reach out to your company with a unified message. You'll need to educate and motivate your co-workers. Don't hide behind a meaningless mission statement or simply throw around a bunch of empty buzzwords. You'll have to back up SCM concepts with action—and cold, hard proof. Measurements will be the lifeblood of your SCM program. Easy-to-understand statistics will demonstrate your program's effectiveness and bring the most jaded employees into the SCM fold.

Your team must never lose sight of this primary objective. Since SCM is not a quick-fix, but a new way of doing business, you'll need to continually sell the program to your company. Shout out the good news with a barrage of reports. Share the credit. Set new goals. It's a group effort and your team will be the cheerleaders.

2. Sell the SCM program to suppliers

Your company and other customers have been beating up your suppliers over price for years. In what has traditionally been an adversarial relationship, you've got to expect a healthy dose of skepticism—even downright mistrust–from suppliers as you propose new SCM alliances. Just as you need to sell the program to your company, you'll have to work hard to win over your suppliers.

And, as with selling SCM to your company, actions will speak louder to suppliers than contrived catch phrases. You've got to "walk the talk." Be fair and consistent. Only when suppliers realize that you're serious about following through will they truly begin to consider Supply Chain Management.

When you help them understand SCM is a "win-win" proposition, suppliers will join the process as full-fledged partners. Again, don't back off from selling the program. It's an ongoing task. When you demonstrate the tangible benefits of continuous improvements, you'll have an SCM partner for the long haul.

3. Develop supplier selection criteria

4. Develop rating system/report card

5. Develop survey/report card

These three steps will comprise the nuts and bolts of your SCM program. Developing and implementing them may appear a bit daunting at first. But as you'll see when we cover these topics in detail later in the book, you've already got many of the components in place. Rest assured, you're not going to completely disregard the policies and procedures you currently use to qualify and evaluate your suppliers. Your assignment won't be to reinvent the wheel so much as aligning all four wheels and getting them headed in the same direction.

Regarding the report cards you will create to rate and survey your suppliers, you will not be issuing simple pass/fail grades. You will generate uncomplicated, yet comprehensive reports that will allow you to examine many performance categories. You'll be able to track trends, pinpoint causes for performance spikes, and provide valuable feedback for both your company and your suppliers. Constant evaluations will keep both you and suppliers on your toes and keep the focus on your mutual quest for continuous improvement.

6. Administer the Supply Chain Management program

Once the components of the program have been developed, the SCM team will oversee its daily management, i.e., capturing and reporting data, sending out supplier report cards, paying suppliers on time, completing supplier corrective actions forms, etc. After the initial curiosity fades away, you'll need to ensure that the program is properly maintained. Sharing performance reports will help keep everyone motivated. Don't forget the team's cheerleading role—it will be just as crucial during SCM's implementation as during its introduction.

Continuity Is Crucial

Ensure that no team members change

After you've assembled the SCM team, you'll want to secure a minimum 18-month commitment from members. It's important to establish a moratorium period so that the team can properly integrate and maintain its momentum. If a team member changes, regression is inevitable as the new member is acclimated. You'll lose valuable time and risk losing credibility as well.

Members will want to resign from the team if they perceive it as a waste of their time. It will be up to your team leaders to make sure that the team is properly empowered and that there is ample delegation of authority among its members. Acknowledge individual members' accomplishments and allow team members to fully share in overall SCM success.

Some companies assure continuity and commitment by linking SCM results to team members' performance reviews. That way, if a member chooses to leave the team, he or she may take a salary hit. Conversely, if SCM goals are reached, it will be reflected in team members' performance reviews. However, be aware of the danger that the team members may compromise the overall SCM program if their salaries are measured against one performance objective. For example, long-term value may suffer when the team is focused only on maximizing profits and lowering costs. Instead, tie performance reviews to multiple criteria such as reducing the supply base, cutting inventory, reducing costs, and improving quality.

SCM Team Meetings

The SCM team will not be effective if meetings are scheduled for only an hour or two each week. Successful programs meet an average of three to four hours per week as the program is getting off the ground. During the start-up phase, the SCM team will be developing the supplier selection criteria, required report cards, audit assessment, and measurements. The allotted three to four hours per week of team meeting time is used as a workshop to develop these elements. In addition, the SCM team must determine how the data is to be collected.

After the program has been established, teams generally meet for three to four hours per month. As the program matures, meeting time will be used to monitor the suppliers' progress and to make sure that supplier report cards are being sent out on time, suppliers are being paid on time, corrective actions are being completed by suppliers, and audit assessment recommendations are being implemented by suppliers.

SCM teams don't fade away. SCM is a never-ending journey. That means your job will never be finished. Your competitors certainly are not going to sit idle. The SCM team can't afford to rest either. Supply Chain Management is not a flavor-of-the-month whim. It's a different way of operating your company. It will require your team's ongoing, concerted effort to maintain its integrity and long-range goals.

Step 2 EXERCISE
Put Your Team Together

Using Figure 2-2, write in who you think would be ideal candidates for your company's Supply Chain Management team. Do some brainstorming; let your mind wander. First determine and prioritize which departments should be represented. Then identify the best representatives from those departments. Remember, there should be between four and seven permanent members on your team. Some departments can assist the team on an as-needed basis.

Seek out senior employees with the most experience. But balance their experience against equally important criteria such as their ability to work cohesively within a group and their attitude towards change. List your first and second choices for each position on your team. Take your time and return to your list periodically to confirm your choices or make changes. This is a critical step in establishing the SCM program at your company. You'll want to be certain that you've recruited the best possible employees for the job.

Who should be on your SCM team?

The "Core Four"		
1 Purchasing		
2 Quality		
3 Manufacturing		
4 Engineering		
The rest of the team		
5 Planning		
6 Cost Accounting		
7 Logistics		
8 Packaging		
9 Research		
10 Sales		
11 Other		

Figure 2-2. *Put your team together.*

Developing Goals and Objectives

" If you don't know where you are going, you will probably end up somewhere else. "

Laurance J. Peter,
The Peter Principle

A few years ago, *Dr. Robert Monczka, a professor of purchasing and materials management at Michigan State's Graduate School of Business, researched the management and procurement strategies of 50 major American manufacturers. Not surprisingly, supplier partnerships figured prominently in their plans. Each company also set aggressive goals for itself. Time and again, wrote Monczka, the same five-year goals showed up in his study:*

- *Year-to-year cost reductions of 5%*

- *Year-to-year quality improvements in the range of 10-15%*

- *A 40-60% reduction in cycle time*

- *Improvement in response to customer wants from 30% to 80%*

Monczka noted that these companies were already winners. Many had shown the ability to improve their quality and processes by a magnitudes of five, eight, or ten. Yet they were the ones challenging themselves by setting the bar ever higher.

Which do you think will yield more success for your company: Setting "impossible" goals and striving to achieve them, although sometimes failing? Or setting timid goals that you can always meet, but that leave you further and further behind your competitors?

Before you go any further, set some specific targets for your Supply Chain Management program. It may seem premature to decide what you're going to accomplish before your program is fully under way, but don't let that stop you. Your determination to set and strive towards specific, ambitious goals is your mark of confidence in your program. In fact, we encourage you to make your goals public. Yes, letting everyone know what you hope to accomplish with SCM increases the risk if you fail, of course. However, going public provides incentive and will add immeasurably to the status of your program when you meet or exceed your goals. If you need a refresher on what you can expect to accomplish with SCM, go back and reread Step 1. For more on goals, take a peak ahead at Step 13.

Step 3 EXERCISE
Setting Your SCM Targets

Every company will have its own reasons for implementing Supply Chain Management. Here are a list of 10 possible goals for an SCM program. Read them over. Select three or four and pencil in some target numbers. Add your own goals if you like. Don't feel that you have to fill them all in, however. This list will begin to give you an idea of what you can achieve. Later, refer back to this page as your program takes shape. As your confidence in SCM grows, you'll be ready to set, and achieve, more ambitious goals.

Establish your SCM goals

#		%
1	Reduce quality defects by	_____ %
2	Reduce early and late deliveries by	_____ %
3	Reduce incoming inspections by	_____ %
4	Reduce rework and scrap by	_____ %
5	Reduce inventory levels by	_____ %
6	Reduce partial receipts by	_____ %
7	Reduce purchase lead times by	_____ %
8	Reduce unplanned downtime by	_____ %
9	Reduce "non-value added" elements by	_____ %
10	Reduce "cost of quality" by	_____ %
11		_____ %
12		_____ %
13		_____ %
14		_____ %
15		_____ %

Figure 3-1. *Determine your Supply Chain Management targets.*

Structuring the Supply Chain

" End the practice of awarding the business on the basis of price tag. Instead, minimize total cost. Move toward a single supplier for any one item, on a long-term relationship of loyalty and trust. "

Dr. W. Edwards Deming

We worked with a world-class manufacturer *of home appliances that had too many suppliers—and they knew it. They even knew how it had happened. The cause was the vicious circle that's all too common in "traditional" procurement practices. Because of late deliveries, partial shipments, quality problems, and general lack of trust in existing suppliers, the purchasing department was always hunting for new suppliers. The more suppliers in the company's corral, the more it could pit them against each other in competition for rock-bottom prices. Suppliers were fighting fiercely for limited business, one purchase order at a time. The result? The appliance manufacturer got its low prices but quality, delivery, and everything else was a mess. Not surprisingly, the suppliers were miserable, too. They were slashing prices to the bone, yet had no assurance of future business and definitely no reason to improve their processes.*

The manufacturer was finally able to remedy the situation when it began to turn suppliers into long-term partners. It has since reduced the number of its electronics suppliers from 25 to six and is continuing to reduce its supply base in other commodities. Most importantly, new suppliers are now developed on the basis of value and speed, not price.

n this section, you'll find out how to choose suppliers with whom
you will enter into a completely different kind of relationship.
Some of the steps will be difficult, and may even seem counter-
intuitive. You can be sure that the process will require diligence
and hard work. Invariably, you'll suffer some setbacks before everything clicks. But you can do it. We'll even go so far as to say that you
must do it. Fortunately, you'll be reaping the rewards long after you've
forgotten the initial discomfort.

A Word about Alliances

"Customer-supplier alliance" may be the most misunderstood, misused
phrase in the whole relationship between manufacturers and their
supply chains. Why? Because nine times out of ten, the person uttering
those words really means either "I need you," or "You need me, so I
own you." In this book, you'll learn how to form customer-supplier
relationships based on equality. These are meaningful alliances,
founded for the mutual benefit of both parties. (Yes, that "win/win"
scenario again.)

Before we go any further, let's address the skeptics who will want to
know how any supplier-purchaser relationship can be based on equality when the partner holding the purse strings has the option of doing
business elsewhere. The simple answer is that in a true customer-supplier alliance, neither party will have the option of going elsewhere, at
least not easily. More importantly, they won't want to. That's because
the partners will have made substantial commitments to each other in
time, dollars, and, most importantly, trust. They won't want to go to
another partner because this unique alliance gives them something they
really can't get elsewhere.

Rest assured, such an alliance is not based on a complete leap of
faith. Before you reach such a deep level of commitment with a supplier, you'll go through a filtering process and a certification process.

In addition, the alliance will be based on maintaining real, measurable standards of performance. The trust will be developed over time. Not all of your existing suppliers will make it but those that do will have earned their place. Nor will it benefit you to hold the power of the purse strings over them. Remember, as always, your goal is value, not price.

Of course, the power can reside with the supplier, too. And, in the case of a sole supplier of a critical commodity, sometimes there isn't much you can do, at least in the short term. In such a case, you're the one saying "I need you." Hopefully, such circumstances are the exception for your company, and not the rule.

Who Do You Want in Your Supply Chain?

Obviously, if you're going to enter into a long-term alliance with a select group of suppliers, you'll want to choose them with some care. In the first part of this chapter, we're going to talk about qualifying suppliers from your existing supplier base. These are the companies you already know. You have a sense of their performance, and can begin to sort them out. At the end of this chapter, we'll discuss bringing in new suppliers, but you'll do that only after you have a supply chain management program in place.

As always, work in manageable steps. To start, your goal will be to bring eight to twelve suppliers into your supply chain management program. Give yourself six months, a year at most, to get comfortable with the process, then bring in another batch of eight to twelve, and so on. You'll be learning the ropes and working out the knots in the first few batches, so they'll be the toughest. Once you have your systems in place and get some experience, the process will go much more smoothly.

Grouping Your Suppliers by Commodity

Before your begin selecting an initial group of suppliers, group your suppliers by commodity or family of parts. That is, gather them in categories such as electronics, plastics, cables, sheet metal, power suppliers, or whatever. Whether you certify suppliers of one commodity at a time, or for several commodities at once, will depend on the experience your supply team members have with those commodities.

Pre-Filtering Your Supplier Pool

For its first substantial assignment, your supply chain team will run existing suppliers through what we call a "pre-filter." Its purpose will be to eliminate companies that have no real chance of qualifying for your supply chain. For one reason or another, they are simply not worth the time, effort, and resources that rating and selecting supplier partners requires. Start with a group of suppliers in one commodity, then rate them according to the elements that follow. Remember, this process just cuts your pool of candidates down to manageable size. The real work lies ahead so don't spend a lot of time here. The three components of the pre-filter are:

    A.   **Dollar volume**

    B.   **Percent of supplier's business**

    C.   **Location**

A.   Dollar volume

Eliminate any supplier not in the top 5% to 20% of your dollar volume per commodity family. That is, if the amount of business you do with suppliers in a commodity family ranges totals $10 million dollars, select only those with whom you spend a half million (5%) to $2 million (20%) annually. Whether you make the cutoff at 5% or closer to 20% will depend largely on how easy it is to pull purchase records on your suppliers. If you can pull the information from a computer fairly quickly, use the top 20%; if you're working by hand, go with a more manageable percentage.

You may have a wonderful supplier who accounts for only $12,000 purchased. Despite stellar performance, such suppliers are generally not worth the effort needed to qualify and audit them. If you can't bear to lose such suppliers, I recommend developing a much simpler performance assessment just for them. Or, you may want to consider increasing the amount of business you do with these suppliers.

B. Percent of supplier's business

Ideally, select for your supplier pool only companies for whom you represent at least 5% to 15%, or more, of their business. That is, you want to be important enough so they'll respond quickly to your requests, particularly for those big favors that involve "jumping" lead times or breaking into their production line. If you find that you must use suppliers for which you represent a minor account (less than 5%), there are three things you can do to boost your success:

- Improve your forecasting: The more advance notice you can give suppliers, the better they'll serve you.

- Share the risk you represent by committing to buy "X" dollars from a supplier over a set period of time.

- Deal with distributors instead of directly with suppliers; let the distributor manage your inventory.

Accommodate as necessary, but even if you represent a relatively small amount of a supplier's business, do not compromise on your standards for quality, quantity, and so forth. If you can abide by the supplier's lead time, then you will still be able to have a very successful SCM program. Conversely, be cautious about having suppliers so dependent upon you that any fluctuation in your order stream puts them in financial jeopardy.

C. Location

You'll have to use your judgment in this area. A supplier should be someone you know well. This means meeting the people you deal with face-to-face on a regular basis and visiting their facility when you need to. In the best case, choose suppliers within a 100-150 miles of your facility. Business is global, however, and many of us have suppliers on the other side of the world. That does not negate the need to know your suppliers thoroughly. We cannot overstate the importance of visiting foreign facilities before signing a contract, and again at regular intervals during the year. One of our pet peeves is the number of companies that refuse to budget travel money for visiting overseas suppliers. This is especially frustrating since companies invariably contract overseas solely for price advantage. Contrary to myth, factors such as quality and delivery are not necessarily superior overseas to what you'll find domestically. Unless you see where that product is coming from and know who you're dealing with, that incremental price advantage can result in a considerable loss in value.

Selecting Your Suppliers

How to choose your partners for a long-term alliance

Once you've identified a pool of suppliers by pre-filtering, you'll focus on narrowing it down to the companies you want to bring into the program. This is the nitty-gritty of the selection process. You won't have a supply chain management program until you pare down the number of your suppliers. Remember, start out qualifying a manageable eight to twelve companies initially.

Identifying Key Selection Criteria

The list shown in Figure 4-1 offers nine criteria for selecting suppliers and blank lines for adding others that you think are appropriate. Each team member should examine the list, with any additional criteria, and rank them from most important to least important. You may be able to accomplish this in one meeting. Or, discuss the list at one meeting, then have team members bring their rankings the next time you assemble. Combine the individual scoring and come up with a final ranking.

There are no right or wrong answers although some items no doubt will appear on everyone's list. Others will depend upon the particular company or industry. Also, a team member from purchasing or quality control will choose differently from an engineer or an accountant. It will be the job of your team to resolve such conflicts and agree on a firm set of selection criteria.

A final word of caution: Don't be overly ambitious in setting criteria. Your goal will be to select just the most important elements from the list. Drop the ones that get the lowest scores. You may end up with seven criteria or as few as three or four. However, if they're far and away the most important, that's fine. You'll have plenty of opportunity to score suppliers on the finer points later in your SCM program. Here, you simply want to bring suppliers into the fold. Keep it simple and keep your SCM program moving so it doesn't lose momentum.

Supplier selection criteria

Rank	Attribute
	Quality
	On-time delivery
	Price competitiveness
	Management behavior
	Technical support
	Correct quantity
	Nearness to plant
	ISO 9000/QS 9000 registration
	SPC

Figure 4-1. *Rank desired supplier attributes.*

Weighting the List

Next, take the criteria you've chosen and rank them from most important to least important. Figure 4-2 uses four criteria as an example: quality, on-time delivery, management behavior, and correct quantity. Each has been assigned a weight, based on its importance. You can extrapolate a weight based on your team's initial ranking of the criteria or you can come up with another system of weighting that better fits your needs. Generally, assign the most important criteria a weight of no more than 40 points, and the least important no less than 10. The weights, you'll notice in this example, add up to 100. This isn't absolutely necessary but you'll be calculating percentages and it will save you a step. Keep it simple. Your team may select different criteria, of course, and assign different weights.

Scoring Your Suppliers

Once you've weighted your list of criteria, score each of your potential suppliers according to the weighted criteria. At this point you're work-

Weighting supplier selection criteria

Criteria	Weight	X	Score	=	Weighted Score
Quality	40	X	90%	=	36.0
On-time delivery	30	X	88%	=	26.4
Correct quantity	20	X	86%	=	17.2
Management behavior	10	X	80%	=	8.0
TOTALS	100				87.6

Figure 4-2. *Multiply to determine a weighted score.*

ing with eight to twelve of your current suppliers. You should be able to construct a performance history on each supplier based on existing data. Understandably, not all the data will be easy to obtain but with a little ingenuity you can do it. That's why this is a team effort.

First, determine how you're going to score each criteria. On quality, we'll score our mythical XYZ Company 3 points for every lot that fully conforms to specifications, 2 points for lots that don't fully meet specs but can be used as is, and 0 points for lots that are rejected or require rework. Since XYZ delivers almost daily, three months of data are sufficient. (For suppliers delivering weekly, use six months history, and for monthly delivery, examine records for about a year.) In the three-month period, XYZ delivered 100 lots. Out of a possible perfect score of 300 (100 lots times 3 points), it earns a score of 270 points, or 90%.

Similarly, your team will generate scores for the other criteria. Again, we urge you to keep things fairly simple. Regarding quantity, based on deliveries of 50 pieces, we'll give 3 points for correct quantity, 2 points for shortages up to 4% or 2 pieces, 1 point for up to 6% or 3 pieces short, and 0 points for more than 3 pieces short. As shown in our example in Figure 4-2, XYZ Company scores 86% on 100 lots.

For on-time delivery, we can score XYZ company 3 points for within 2 days of scheduled delivery, 2 points for 3 to 4 days early or late, 1 point for 5 to 6 days off schedule, and 0 points for any greater deviation from schedule. If early delivery doesn't adversely affect your operation, you can score early deliveries the same as on time. We'll give XYZ Company an on-time delivery score of 88% for 100 lots.

Scoring "Soft" Criteria

You may wonder how to go about assigning a numerical score to an attribute like management behavior. Actually, it's easier than you think. First, set up a simple scoring system, such as:

Excellent = 3	Good = 2
Fair = 1	Poor = 0

Then, sit down with your team and brainstorm a series of questions that reflect what you expect from the management of your supplier companies. In this case, we suggest that "management" refer only to the people at the facility with which you do business, not at some remote corporate level. The facility you deal with is where you want responsive management and that's where your feedback can make a difference.

Figure 4-3 offers five sample questions regarding management

Scoring management behavior

	Score	Behavior
1	2	Does supplier's management respond quickly to problems?*
2	3	Is supplier's management fair in negotiations?
3	2	Does supplier's management solve problems quickly and fairly?
4	3	Does supplier's management identify opportunities to improve quality and on-time delivery as well as reduce costs?
5	2	Does supplier's management have an effective corrective action program?
	12	XYZ Company total score
		Total possible score (100%) = 15
		XYZ Company = 80%

*You can be even more specific, e.g.:
Score 3 if within 24 hours
Score 2 if less than 48 hours
Score 1 if less than 3 days
Score 0 if over 3 days

Figure 4-3. *Develop your list of management expectations.*

behavior to get you started. You'll find others in Step 6. In a team meeting, you can probably generate at least 25 more with no trouble. Once you've established the questions, rate the management of your suppliers according to our scale, then assign a percentage based on how close they came to a perfect score, as we did for quality, quantity, and on-time delivery.

Ranking the Suppliers

Once you've completed scoring a company based on your criteria, as shown in Figure 4-1, add up the weighted scores and calculate the percentage for that company. In our example, since a perfect score equals 100, the XYZ Company's "grade" is 87.6%. If your scoring base is other than 100, you'll have to go through an extra step to get a percentage. Grade the suppliers in your selection pool and compare grades, e.g.:

> ABC Company   92%
>
> LMN Company   81.5%
>
> XYZ Company   87.6%

You now have a comparison of your suppliers based on hard data. It's simply a matter of selecting the suppliers you need based on the scores.

How Many Suppliers Should You Have?

Remember, one of the goals of supply chain management is to reduce your supplier base. Traditional purchasing wisdom teaches that the more suppliers the better. That way, you can pit one against the other to get the best price. However, we're interested in the new way. We know that focusing on price alone rarely produces the best value. In supply chain management, we want to reduce the number of suppliers and work on enhancing the relationship with those that remain. On the next page are some considerations that may affect the number of companies in your supply base:

The Need to Sustain Competition

Although the objective is not to pit suppliers against each other in price wars, it is healthy to have them competing on quality and technology. Depending upon the nature of the products you're purchasing, therefore, keep a "critical mass" of suppliers in certain commodity families.

The Depth of a Supplier's Product Range

Your supply needs may be too broad for a few suppliers to cover. Or, you may have highly qualified suppliers with a limited product range.

The Complexity of Your Products

The greater the complexity of your products, the greater the number of commodity families from which you'll be purchasing and the greater the number of individual suppliers. For example, in the article cited at the beginning of Step 1, Chrysler had reduced its supplier base by more than half, yet still had more than 1,100 suppliers.

How Many Suppliers for Each Commodity Family?

Related to the preceding section is the question of how many suppliers you should have per commodity family. Plotting your supplier base by commodity family will be a good exercise for your team. For each family, simply list the active suppliers for the past 12 or 18 months. Based on what we've covered so far, make an educated guess about the number of suppliers you will actually need. Do this during your initial supplier selection process, then at least once a year thereafter.

Remember, your goal is to reduce the number of suppliers. If you're currently using five suppliers in a commodity family, ask why that number shouldn't be four, or three, or even one. Many companies that adopt Supply Chain Management have slashed their supply base by 50-80% in the first two to three years. If you can't reduce your company's supply base in a commodity family by at least 20% in the first year, you're just not trying hard enough! You can do it.

Bringing in New Suppliers

So far, we've only been talking about our existing suppliers. Now, let's look at the issue of bringing in new suppliers. When and how should you bring in new suppliers? The best, answer is: **no new suppliers**.

Realistically, however, there will always be some exceptions. You may be launching a new design for which you don't have an existing supplier. Or, your output may be growing and you need more capacity than your suppliers can meet. However, even in such cases, we recommend going to existing suppliers and working with them to add the needed commodity to their product line or to boost their capacity. If you're a good customer, and you have a mutually beneficial long-term relationship, it will be in your common interest if the supplier can meet your needs.

Notice that we haven't mentioned price. However, in the real world, you will inevitably be approached by companies promising to beat your existing suppliers on price while matching them on quality, delivery, and anything else you can think of. What should you do?

This is a delicate issue. If you've spent many hours and a lot of work building up a credible relationship with your existing suppliers based on value, not price, you instantly destroy that credibility when you jump to a new supplier who promises to save you two cents an item. However, every company is going to have a price point that it just cannot ignore. Here's what to do when you hit yours:

For starters, **do not** qualify a potential supplier on "first article." It should be no surprise a company's first output will be perfect. Instead, notify the company that you'll be doing a rigorous assessment to ensure that your standards will be met. Then, do it, and don't compromise.

Send a team to the facility to do an intensive capability study. Your goal will be to discover how they match up with your existing suppliers on quality, delivery, quantity, lead time, backlog, etc. Your assessment team should have a business agent, who will understand the candidate's costing, as well as technical and production people who can meaningfully assess production capabilities. (For a detailed description of supplier assessments, see Steps 6 and 9.)

Naturally, this kind of scrutiny requires a supplier who will practically open the books for your inspection team. However, quality suppliers will expect to do so. If you're denied access to pertinent information, a warning flag should go up immediately.

Then, only when you're satisfied that the new supplier can meet your current suppliers' capabilities on the full range of factors, should you look at price. If you do make a decision to go with a new supplier, you should feel confident justifying your decision to existing suppliers. On the other hand, if current suppliers are jumping through hoops to meet your SCM standards and the word gets out that another company snuck in on price alone, you'll undo a lot of hard work and good will.

Designating Supplier Tiers

Many exemplary companies sort their qualified suppliers into tiers as shown in Figure 4-4. In the chart, **qualified** companies meet the minimum standard for certification and **preferred** companies are superior to those. The **certified** designation is often reserved for a select few companies. For instance, you might specify that only the suppliers with whom you do the top 5% in dollar volume can become certified. That doesn't mean they're automatically certified because they send you big invoices! It simply means that only suppliers at that level of spending can earn the highest designation. They must still qualify on merit. And, they must earn certification in all categories. However, once they achieve certification, you'll look to them first when new opportunities arise. Likewise, preferred suppliers will get new business before qualified suppliers.

The Next Step

Congratulations! By the time your team completes the supplier selection process your supply chain management program will be well on the way to success. You've selected a core group of suppliers with whom you can begin to work. The next few chapters will discuss monitoring and improving their ongoing performance. About six months after you've selected the first group, begin bringing in your next group. Then another group six months after that, and so on. Yes, it's a lot of work, but it gets easier. And, as we mentioned at the beginning, SCM produces results. You'll soon be showing real, measurable gains as a direct result of your program. Support for your SCM program *will* grow.

Supplier Tier Chart

Element	Certified	Preferred	Qualified
Quality	100%	98% to 100%	95% to 97%
On-time delivery	100%±1 day	100%±2 days	100%±3 days
Quantity accuracy	100%±2%	100%±5%	100%±10%
Quality survey	90%	80%	70%

Figure 4-4. *Determine certification levels.*

Step 4 EXERCISE
Ranking Your Suppliers

In this exercise, you'll compare the performance of three suppliers over the past six months. First, assign a percentage score to companies A, B, and C based on the performance data in Figure 4-5. The score for quality has already been completed. In Figure 4-6, use the percentages from Figure 4-5 to calculate the weighted scores for each company. The total weighted scores will enable you to compare the three companies.

Performance data

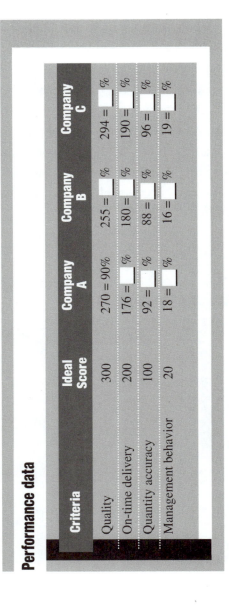

Criteria	Ideal Score	Company A	Company B	Company C
Quality	300	270 = 90%	255 = ___%	294 = ___%
On-time delivery	200	176 = ___%	180 = ___%	190 = ___%
Quantity accuracy	100	92 = ___%	88 = ___%	96 = ___%
Management behavior	20	18 = ___%	16 = ___%	19 = ___%

Figure 4-5. *Determine percentages.*

Weighted scores

Company A						
Criteria	**Weight**	**X**	**Score**		**=**	**Weighted Score**
Quality	40	X	90%		=	36
On-time delivery	30	X	☐	%	=	☐
Quantity accuracy	20	X	☐	%	=	☐
Management behavior	10	X	☐	%	=	☐
TOTALS	100					☐

Company B						
Criteria	**Weight**	**X**	**Score**		**=**	**Weighted Score**
Quality	40	X	☐	%	=	☐
On-time delivery	30	X	☐	%	=	☐
Quantity accuracy	20	X	☐	%	=	☐
Management behavior	10	X	☐	%	=	☐
TOTALS	100					☐

Company C						
Criteria	**Weight**	**X**	**Score**		**=**	**Weighted Score**
Quality	40	X	☐	%	=	☐
On-time delivery	30	X	☐	%	=	☐
Quantity accuracy	20	X	☐	%	=	☐
Management behavior	10	X	☐	%	=	☐
TOTALS	100					☐

Figure 4-6. *Enter the performance data from Figure 4-5, then multiply to determine the weighted scores for these companies.*

Developing Your Report Card Rating System

" In God we trust; all others must bring data. *"*

Unfortunately, most current supplier evaluation systems *are disjointed. Purchasing systems track purchase order prices, delivery prices, lead times, and delivery. Quality assurance systems analyze pieces or lots accepted, rejected, and corrected. What companies need is a more sophisticated holistic evaluation program that integrates both cost and quality performance measurements.*

Rockwell International Corporation's Supplier Rating and Incentive Program (SRIP) is one of the best approaches to a comprehensive measurement system. Implemented in 1986, Rockwell's SRIP program brings its suppliers' quality and cost considerations together in an exhaustive report card format. Nothing is left to conjecture; all relevant performance factors are supported by hard data. Rockwell's purchase orders are now awarded based on total cost.

Rockwell used to characterize itself as a premier supplier of high-priced, high-quality military electronic systems. But, to stay competitive, Rockwell learned that it had to offer the lowest total cost, best value, and highest quality. Through its SRIP program, Rockwell works with its suppliers to eliminate any costs that do not add quality to the final product. Today, Rockwell is a transformed company.

SRIP has been adopted by Motorola, Hamilton Standard, Honeywell, Ford Aerospace, General Dynamics, Hughes Aircraft, Litton Data Systems, Sunstrand, Simmons Precision, and Northrop.

f Supply Chain Management is a quality journey, then report cards will be the snapshots you take along the way. They will offer a compelling record of where you and your suppliers travel in your mutual quest for quality. By capturing a supplier's performance over a period of time, you'll be able to document its successes (and failures) in meeting the goals you set. You will better understand how your suppliers compare to one another. And you will get an objective, true sense of the impact your suppliers have on your bottom line.

The rating systems covered in this chapter will be the heart of your SCM program. They will provide constant feedback to both you and your suppliers. When designed and managed properly, report cards will give your suppliers incentives to excel.

You will need to generate hard, measurable data for all report card elements. These will not be simple "yes" and "no" or "pass" and "fail" checklists. While some of the sub-categories you will include in your report cards may be qualitative, you will develop numeric, quantitative rating values, much as we did for the "soft" criteria in the previous chapter.

There are two basic types of SCM report cards: **trends** and **best supplier**. Trends report cards measure an individual supplier's performance against itself. Usually issued monthly, but sometimes weekly or even daily, a trends report card illustrates whether a supplier is improving, regressing, or staying the same. A best supplier report card, as its name implies, pulls together data from many suppliers to compare and contrast their performances.

Share your trends report cards with your suppliers. However you will generally keep best supplier cards internally. If you do release them, you should anonymously list the suppliers as "Company A," "Company B," etc. Nonetheless, if your suppliers have done their homework, they will probably be able to determine their competitors' identities. Best supplier report cards will usually include an average of your suppliers' performance data taken over a six- or twelve-month span. Typically, trends report cards will reflect a rolling 12-month period.

Be careful not to unduly penalize a supplier who may experience a serious but short-lived problem. The anomaly could skew the data. For a more accurate picture, look at best supplier cards in tandem with each supplier's trends report during the same period. A steady, but mediocre, supplier may score higher overall than one who suffers a temporary irregularity. However, your SCM program may be better, in the long run, with a supplier who demonstrates the willingness and ability to work with you to resolve an issue.

The Elements of Your SCM Report Cards

The elements you will choose to include in your rating system, and the weight you will assign to each one, will depend upon the nature of your business, the types of suppliers with whom you work, and the scope of the products or services they produce for you. The majority of SCM

SCM report cards typically measure these elements and assign these relative weights

Element	Points
Quality: Material acceptance	50
Delivery: On-time and complete	30
Cost & Service	20
Total points	100

Figure 5-1. *In general, assign quality the highest weight.*

programs, however, include these three categories: **quality**, **delivery**, and **cost & service**.

Figure 5-1 shows the rating elements and the allocated points for a typical SCM report card. As we have been saying all along, price, the traditional standard for measuring suppliers, is not the primary focus in a Supply Chain Management program. For this example, "cost & service" trails a distant third. Quality, generally measured as material acceptance, is fully one-half of the score. Delivery accounts for about one-third of the points. When measuring delivery, you will want to look at both whether a supplier's products arrive on time (early deliveries are often penalized along with late deliveries) and if they are complete. The cost and service element might include sub-categories such as the cost of carrying a supplier's safety inventory and the supplier's ability to reduce lead times.

Measuring Quality

In order to measure quality, you will need to establish protocols for your material acceptance. You don't necessarily have to reinvent the wheel. If you already have a successful QC program in place, you may simply need to assign numeric values and set up a data recording system. There are three quality measurement systems you can adopt:

- **Percent lots accepted**
- **Percent pieces accepted**
- **Defects per million (DPM)**

It does not matter which system you choose for your SCM report cards but, to ensure consistency, you should use the same criteria for all suppliers within the same commodity group.

With percent lots accepted, you will either approve or reject entire lots. If a lot is 100% accepted, you will award full value for that lot. In Figure 5-2, each accepted lot would receive 100 points. If QC rejects a lot but your company chooses to use as is (UAI), the lot will score lower. For the example in Figure 5-2, a rejected UAI lot would receive

50 points, or one-half of the points awarded for an accepted lot. A "use-as-is" situation might arise with defects that are largely cosmetic but would not affect the integrity of your finished product.

In other cases, a company might reject lots and return them to the supplier to be reworked (RWK). Finally, a company might outright return lots with serious defects to the supplier (RTS). Whether a rejected lot falls into the UAI, RWK, or RTS category often depends on how badly the company needs the parts. (When you prepare your quality rating system, you should substitute inspection language which your company or industry regularly uses.) In Figure 5-2, the company would not award any points for rejected RWK or RTS lots. Using percent lots accepted, the example shows how a company would arrive at a rating of 80 (out of a possible 100) for a supplier who shipped 15 lots during a sample one-month period. In this example, the supplier's overall monthly report card (measuring quality, delivery, and cost & service)

Material acceptance rating

Lot Status	Points per Lot	No. Lots for Month	Total Points
100% Quality-accepted	100	10	1000
Lots rejected, UAI	50	4	200
Lots rejected, RWK	0	1	0
Lots rejected, RTS	0	0	0
TOTALS		15	1200

Quality formula:

$$\frac{\text{Total Points}}{\text{No. Lots}} = \frac{1200}{15} = 80$$

Figure 5-2. *This is an example of measuring quality by using percent of material lots accepted. The rating is based on a supplier which delivered 15 lots during the month.*

would reflect a quality score of 40 points or 80% of the total possible 50 quality points.

In the percent pieces accepted model, your company's QC team would sample a fixed number of individual pieces within each lot. Whatever percentage of pieces (total pieces accepted divided by total pieces received) you accept during the report card's rating period will become the quality rating for that supplier. For example, if you accept 84% of the pieces received during a month, the supplier's quality rating would be 84 for that report card. Transferring this rating to the overall monthly report card, the supplier would receive 84% of the total possible 50 quality points or a quality score of 42 points.

Larger organizations might choose the defects-per-million (DPM) system. In order to assign numeric values, companies need to benchmark industry standards for the targeted supply. For example, a defect rate of zero to 100 parts per million inspected might be considered world class for a certain item. A rate in this range might warrant a score of 100 points. DPM of 101 to 250 might yield a score of 90 points while a supplier would receive 80 points for 251 to 600 DPM. If anything greater than 600 DPM falls considerably below best-of-industry performance, the company would not award any points in this example

Evaluating Delivery

What is on-time delivery? That's a question your SCM team will have to answer for each commodity group your company receives. What flow of supplies do you require to properly run your business? What are the supply quantity tolerance levels you need to maintain? The goal will be to eliminate overages and shortages within reasonable parameters. Once you can count on your suppliers for accurate and steady delivery, you will be able to reduce or do away with safety stock. You will generally break your SCM report card's delivery rating down into two sub-elements: an on-time rating and a quantity complete rating.

Some companies set delivery windows as tight as ten minutes! In this case, the company would record on a supplier's report card any lots which are received more than ten minutes late or ten minutes early. In most cases, a delivery window of days makes more sense.

Figure 5-3 illustrates how a company would arrive at an on-time rating of 72 for a supplier who shipped 15 lots in a monthly reporting period. It may be tempting to award 100 points to suppliers whose lots are received zero to two days early and no points for all other

On-time delivery rating

Lot Status	Points per Lot	No. Lots for Month	Total Points
0 to 2 days early	100	5	500
3 to 4 days early	75	4	300
5 to 6 days early	50	3	150
7 to 8 days early	25	0	0
9 or more days early	0	0	0
1 to 2 days late	75	0	0
3 to 4 days late	50	2	100
5 to 6 days late	25	1	25
7 or more days late	0	0	0
Totals		15	1075

On-Time Rating:

$$\frac{\text{Total Points}}{\text{No. Lots}} = \frac{1075}{15} = 72$$

Figure 5-3. *This is a sample on-time delivery report card. The rating is based on a supplier which delivered 15 lots during the month.*

deliveries. But that would penalize suppliers who deliver lots eleven days late as harshly as those who deliver lots three days early. You'll be able to generate a more meaningful delivery picture with more discrete on-time rating levels.

Systemic tolerance for lot overages has led to widespread supplier abuse. If a supplier knows that your company will readily accept a 10% overrun, you can expect a never-ending stream of 10% overages. While

Quantity-complete delivery rating

Lot Status	Points per Lot	No. Lots for Month	Total Points
0 to 2% quantity over	100	5	500
3 to 4% quantity over	75	2	150
5 to 6% quantity over	50	1	50
7 to 8% quantity over	25	0	0
9% or more quantity over	0	0	0
1 to 2% quantity short	75	0	0
3 to 4% quantity short	50	4	200
5 to 6% quantity short	25	3	75
7% or more quantity short	0	0	0
Totals		15	975

Quantity complete rating:

$$\frac{\text{Total Points}}{} = \frac{975}{} = 65$$

Figure 5-4. *This is a sample quantity-complete delivery report card. The rating is based on a supplier which delivered 15 lots during the month.*

quantity control can never be perfect, you will want to narrow under-runs and overruns as much as possible. The percent levels you will establish will depend upon the supply's unit cost and its impact on your bottom line. A 5% overage on a low ticket item is not as critical as a 3% overage on a higher-priced supply. Figure 5-4 shows how a company would arrive at a quantity-complete rating of 65 for a supplier who shipped 15 lots in a monthly reporting period.

As your SCM program matures and your suppliers' on-time deliveries improve, you will want to reduce your delivery windows. Eventually, you should be able to establish same-day delivery as a given. You may even want to explore narrowing your windows down to hours or, yes, even minutes if your company is engaged in a continuous or repetitive process.

Because so much is at stake for your suppliers, your SCM program, and your company, make sure that your on-time delivery data—indeed, all of your SCM data—is accurate. Collect information daily and bring your MIS department into the process. If your MIS team has a backlog of pending projects, consider entering the data into a spreadsheet program on a PC.

Evaluating Cost & Service

Unlike delivery and quality, cost & service can be a bit more elusive to measure. You will want to develop sub-elements that correspond to your suppliers and your company. Some of the categories that generally fall under cost & service include:

- Cost of carrying inventory
- Performance vs. price target
- Cost reduction to target
- Lead time reduction
- Corrective action program
- Response time to failure analysis
- Product packaging to specifications
- Design support

The first four elements listed above are hard measurements. You should be able to generate objective data to support your rating. The other categories are more qualitative. You'll need to develop a rating system that equates points with judgments such as "excellent," "acceptable," etc.

In some cases, collecting cost & service data will require a great deal of work on your SCM team's part. Producing SCM report cards should not be a hollow exercise. Be prudent. The number of categories you choose to include in your cost & service rating and the relative weight you assign to each one will be determined by the value the measurements bring to your organization.

Producing and Using SCM Report Cards

Pulling all the information together

You've established the elements of your rating system. You have broken down the elements into sub-categories. You've collected data. Now it's time to gather all of your data and create the actual report cards.

Figure 5-5 shows a trend report card for a new SCM program. This card covers a three-month period. Once your program matures, you will want your trend report cards to reflect rolling twelve-month periods. Note that the elements and the total rating improve each month. Considering these numbers, the company is justified in increasing its percentage of business and dollar volume with this supplier.

Who should get your SCM trend report cards? Within your company, you will want to circulate the document fairly widely. As noted earlier in the chapter, you'll also want to distribute the trend report card to suppliers. Be sure to send them to the highest-ranking people at your suppliers' plants, such as the president or general manager. Forward copies to the quality manager and the customer service manager, as well. Although a supplier's sales force will probably express the greatest desire for your SCM trend report cards, they have the least to offer you in return. They will want to use the information to encourage more sales (assuming the reports are positive) but they typically have little influence on the plant floor.

If a supplier's performance remains flat or declines, you can assume that its management does not care about your SCM program and does not value your business. If that is the case, your account is probably too small a part of its business. You will be better off finding a supplier that will appreciate your account more because it represents a significant portion of its business.

Other suppliers who truly do value your business may think that your SCM program will be a passing fad. Since they hope it will just go away, they may not act to improve their performance. When they see

Trend report card

Element	Max. Points	Jan.	Feb.	March
Quality	50	45	46	47
Delivery	30	27	27	28
Cost & service	20	15	15	16
Totals	100	87	88	91
% of business		80%	82%	85%
$ volume		250K	275K	300K
Quantity		5000	5200	5500
# deliveries		15	15	16

Figure 5-5. *This is a sample supplier trend report card. The card covers a three-month reporting period.*

that you really will reward business based on SCM report card ratings, they will change their behavior.

Companies that have established long-standing relationships with suppliers through mature SCM programs may be able to improve quality and delivery to the point that they no longer need to measure either. Such companies can then focus on more subtle supplier elements, such as engineering innovation or communications.

A sample comparison report card is shown in Figure 5-6. Each supplier's ratings are averages of the previous rolling 12-month period. Just as suppliers may be slow to act once they receive SCM trend report cards, some companies may initially ignore comparison report cards. In Figure 5-6, supplier C is clearly under-performing. Yet a com-

Supplier comparison report card

Element	Max. Points	Supplier A	Supplier B	Supplier C
Quality	50	45	40	30
Delivery	30	25	20	10
Cost & service	20	15	13	10
Totals	100	85	73	50
% of business		60%	30%	10%
$ volume		250K	135K	40K
Quantity		5000	2200	100
# deliveries		15	15	16

Figure 5-6. *This is a sample supplier comparison report card. The element values are averages based on a twelve-month reporting period.*

pany may choose to do nothing in the hope that the supplier will "turn around." Maybe the company has been working with the supplier for a long time and personal relationships are standing in the way of sound business practice.

Remember that one of the primary goals of Supply Chain Management will be to reduce your supply base. Shrinking the supply base will drive down your cost and improve your efficiencies. Comparison report cards will give you the information to eliminate suppliers objectively. Act on it!

It comes down to your company's long-term commitment to Supply Chain Management. If you are truly in it for the long haul, you will use the information in your SCM report cards to guide your alliances with suppliers. If you demonstrate your resolve, your suppliers will respond accordingly; quality, delivery and other elements will improve and your competitive edge will sharpen.

Step 5 EXERCISE
Fill Out Report Cards

Using Figure 5-7, determine each of the four month's total supplier trend ratings for Suppliers A, B, and C. Then calculate a four-month average for each of the supplier's elements and enter this data in the supplier comparison report card. Using the information in the trend and comparison report cards, make some recommendations about modifying the amount of business with each supplier.

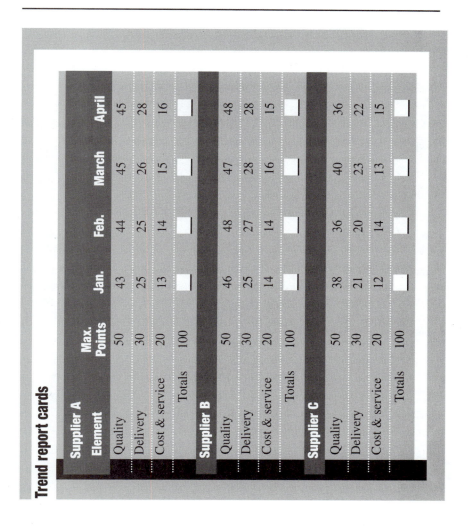

Figure 5-7. *Add the elements together for suppliers A, B, and C and fill in the missing totals. Use this information to complete the exercise in Figure 5-8.*

Supplier comparison report card

Element	Max. Points	Supplier A	Supplier B	Supplier C
Quality	50	☐	☐	☐
Delivery	30	☐	☐	☐
Cost & service	20	☐	☐	☐
Totals	100	☐	☐	☐

Figure 5-8. *Determine averages for each element based on the four-month period from the trend report cards in Figure 5-7 and enter the information above. Considering the trend and comparison report cards, what recommendations would you make to this company about modifying the amount of business it conducts with Supplier A? How about Supplier B? Supplier C?*

STEP 6

Developing a Tactical Supply Chain Assessment

" Crafty men condemn studies; simple men admire them; wise men use them. *"*

"Know your suppliers"—*that's one lesson we can't overstate. The necessity for hard information about suppliers is dramatically illustrated in the book,* Car: A Drama of the American Workplace, *by Mary Walton (W.W. Norton & Co.). A key section recounts the trials Ford endured when it outsourced the seats for the redesigned Ford Taurus.*

According to the book, after signing a multi-million dollar, multi-year contract with Lear, a seat manufacturer, the Taurus design team discovered that the company was woefully unprepared for the job. As production dates loomed, seats arrived at the Ford plant with back panels falling off, defective recliner handles, seams ripping open, and other significant problems. With no alternative supplier, Ford had no choice but to pressure Lear. The problems were eventually fixed, but at a tremendous cost to both parties in money and stress.

One paragraph revealed the root of the problems: "Even a cursory investigation by Ford would have revealed that Lear had a shortage of engineering talent....The first year [Ford's seat supervisor] had worked on seats as a young engineer, the supervisor entrusted him with only a plastic part and a couple of screws. It took him three years to get to a front seat. But Lear was hiring green college graduates who barely knew a bolster from a bezel. They couldn't even do an engineering drawing, so changes weren't documented. They were evasive when asked about stress tests."

All of that time, expense, and anxiety could have been avoided by performing a fairly simple supplier assessment. Remember, even the toughest contracts negotiated by the biggest companies are no substitute for hard information about a supplier.

I n the previous step, we discussed supplier report cards—tools to evaluate and compare suppliers based on information you collect at your loading dock (or at least at arm's length). In this section, the focus is on developing a way to measure and compare your suppliers from a much closer perspective.

The Tactical Supply Chain Assessment enables you to peer into your suppliers' inner workings. It provides the information you need to work with suppliers on improving their processes and to ensure that you get the quality, delivery, and price you need to stay competitive. It's a powerful instrument crucial to developing great suppliers.

In this section, you'll begin to design an assessment instrument that meets the specific needs of your company. In Step 9, you'll learn about going out to your suppliers' facilities to perform assessments.

Assessing, or auditing, your suppliers helps you determine how well they do the things that are most important to your company. Specifically, a supplier assessment identifies:

1. How the supplier performs relative to other suppliers and to the marketplace
2. The commitment of the supplier's management to your company
3. The supplier's capabilities and deficiencies
4. Opportunities for improvement in the supplier's operations
5. The supplier's willingness to improve

Who To Assess

A Tactical Supply Chain Assessment continues the supplier selection process discussed in Step 4. However, supplier assessments are much more thorough. They're also relatively time-consuming. To administer them, a team from your company spends several days at the supplier's facility. Because of the time involved, most companies just won't find it practical to perform an assessment on every supplier, and certainly not right away.

A good rule of thumb is to perform supplier assessments on the top 5% of your suppliers in the first six months or year. Then, do the next 15%. When you have assessed 20% of your supply base, you will have covered your biggest, most important suppliers. Repeat assessments on a regular cycle of six months or a year.

You may not need to do full assessments on more than your top 20%. At the end of Step 9, we discuss ways to assess smaller suppliers that don't warrant a full assessment. Ultimately, the number of assessments performed will depend on management's commitment and your total number of suppliers.

Assessing New Suppliers

Another key use for the supplier assessment is to screen new suppliers, as mentioned in Step 4. There's an almost irresistible temptation, as we've mentioned, to take the bait when a supplier dangles a lower price than you're currently paying. Wouldn't it be better to first find out what is attached to the bait? A supplier assessment can help determine whether a low-price supplier is offering a sweetened, and deceptive, price or real value. We recommend that you require a full assessment of any supplier with whom you have the potential to do business at or above a specified dollar amount. For example, if you spend $100,000 or more with each of the top 20% of your suppliers, then assess any new supplier competing for that amount of business.

Elements to assess in a tactical supply chain assessment

	Element	What to Look For
1	Management Behavior	• Management's commitment to quality • Management ensures internal audits are performed • Management provides training programs
2	Quality Practices	• Quality system documented • Continuous quality improvement philosophy exists • System to evaluate cost of non-conformance implemented
3	Procurement	• Quality history considered along with delivery and cost • Purchased material requirements adequately specified • SPC used to track sub-suppliers
4	Materials	• Incoming material identified and controlled • Production material identified and traceable • Non-conforming material segregated, documented, and controlled
5	Manufacturing	• Manufacturing process changes controlled • Inspections and tests performed at appropriate points • Preventive maintenance implemented

Figure 6-1. *Assess these elements and look for these characteristics.*

Elements to assess in a tactical supply chain assessment

(continued)

	Element	What to Look For
6	Design Information	• Control of documents and design changes • Customer specs available to procurement and manufacturing • Critical characteristics defined
7	Statistical Techniques	• Supplier utilizes analytical techniques • Appropriate statistical techniques applied for process control • Capabilities of critical processes and machines monitored
8	Calibration	• Effective calibration program exists • Use of non-calibrated equipment prohibited • Repeatability of measuring devices established

Figure 6-1. *(continued)*

Designing Your Supply Chain Assessment

Supplier assessments are unique to each company. The questions in your assessment tool must reflect the needs of your company. At the end of this chapter we've attached a portion of a supplier assessment. It will give you a framework for designing or expanding your company's assessment. We strongly caution you NOT simply to use it as is. Developing your own assessment is hard work, but it will guarantee that you collect meaningful information that you can really use. It will also ensure that you're clear about the action you want the supplier to take in response to each question. The information that follows will help you to design the right assessment for your company.

Identifying the Elements to Assess

The first step in designing your assessment is to determine what should be measured. The table shown in Figure 6-1 lists eight of the most common elements to assess. The right-hand column breaks down each area into measurable specifics.

This is just an example. Many of these areas are important to every company, others less so. For example, number 7, Statistical Techniques, may not be an issue for your company. Or you may want to bundle it under item 5, Manufacturing. You also may want to add more elements, depending upon your company and industry. Try to avoid getting too detailed, though. Over-designing your assessment can result in gathering reams of difficult-to-use information. As we'll discuss in more detail later, the best strategy is to keep your assessment tool fairly general, but to select a knowledgeable team to administer it.

Developing the Supplier Assessment Questions

We assume that most companies have some means of evaluating suppliers. The examples shown in Figure 6-2 and at the end of the chapter will help you expand or reformulate your supplier evaluation. What we want to stress is the importance of measuring degrees of conformance to standards. With that kind of information, you can find real solutions and begin the process of continuous improvement. Avoid "yes/no" and "pass/fail" questions. On the other hand, avoid scoring that attempts to split hairs. Your assessment team can waste a lot of time quibbling over whether a supplier's procurement system deserves to be scored as a 7 or an 8 on a scale of 1 to 10.

The members of your supply chain management team or assessment team should be responsible for overseeing the design of the assessment

Category 1: Management behavior

1.3 Management is responsible for performing internal quality system audits to verify system conformance

0 Points	• No internal audits are performed
1 Point	• Internal quality system audits are conducted but no corrective action is evident
2 Points	• Internal audits are scheduled annually and performed with defined reports and distributions • Corrective action plans are required for internal audits
3 Points	• Internal audits are scheduled semi-annually and performed with defined reports and distributions • There is a documented procedure for conducting internal quality audits • There is defined responsibility for conducting audits • There is a detailed system for verifying effectiveness of corrective action
4 Points	• Internal audits are scheduled quarterly and performed with defined reports and distributions • Internal audit evaluates effectiveness of activity as well as conformance to procedure • Management reviews are conducted on results of audits

Figure 6-2. *Sample element from a supply chain evaluation.*

form according to their areas of expertise. They're the experts. A purchasing person can best determine what constitutes an adequate procurement system.

Figure 6-2 shows one question series from an assessment of management behavior. Specifically, it assesses management's commitment to internal audits. The sample shows five behaviors worth from 0 to 4 points. Note that points are awarded on the basis of specific actions or requirements, not on qualitative, subjective evaluations. In this case, a supplier would have to score at least a 2 to earn a "passing" grade.

You can also include questions designed to elicit answers that fall within a range. However, range scoring can lead you into the trap of requiring many questions in order to cover all the possibilities inherent in a situation. Two examples of range scoring:

Q: The company has documented procedures for storage, control, and release of all materials: ___

Rating	Points
Excellent	3
Acceptable	2
Deficiencies	1
Unacceptable	0

Q: There is prompt communication between the supplier and customer if non-conforming products or materials are discovered or suspected: ___

Rating	Points
Always	3
Sometimes	2
Rarely	1
Never	0

There will be a temptation to have every system up to date and perfect in your own company before you begin evaluating your suppliers on the same areas. That will endlessly delay your assessment, however, and it's simply not necessary. For example, assess your suppliers' internal quality audit systems while you're still developing your system. You'll make more progress, you'll better understand your suppliers' needs in that area, and you'll learn together.

The number of items or questions you arrive at in your completed assessment will vary depending upon the needs of your company or industry. Again, don't go overboard. We have reviewed and worked with supplier assessments from companies in many industries and believe a world-class assessment requires no more than 40 to 50 question series of the type shown in example 6-2. An assessment with 200 questions, on the other hand, will boggle the mind of everyone involved and will probably cause as many problems as it solves.

Testing Your Assessment Tool

We recommend performing a dry run or pilot test with your assessment tool, either by assessing your own departments or by assessing the facility of a nearby supplier. The goal of the test is to see how well the assessment tool works and to allow time for modification and fine tuning. Look for sections with too much ambiguity in the scoring and others that can be simplified without compromising your ability to collect useful information. A test also gives your assessment team an opportunity to become familiar with using the form.

Step 6 EXAMPLE
Tactical Supply Chain Assessment

The next few pages provide an example of an assessment of a supplier's management behavior. This assessment is based on our work with a number of companies in different industries. Note that, as discussed earlier in the chapter, it uses only five gradations of behavior and they are based on specific actions. The value to you will depend on your company, the industry you're in, and the kind of suppliers you use.

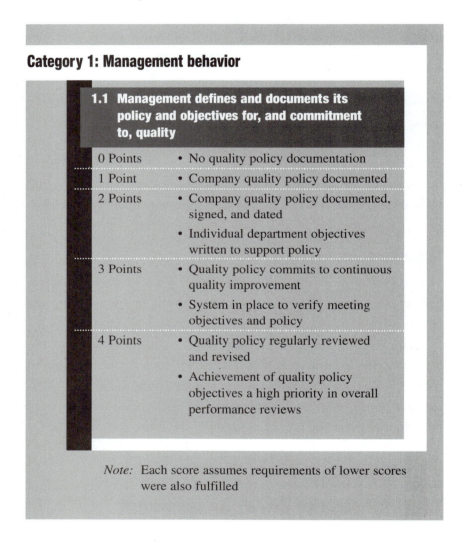

Category 1: Management behavior

1.1 Management defines and documents its policy and objectives for, and commitment to, quality

0 Points	• No quality policy documentation
1 Point	• Company quality policy documented
2 Points	• Company quality policy documented, signed, and dated
	• Individual department objectives written to support policy
3 Points	• Quality policy commits to continuous quality improvement
	• System in place to verify meeting objectives and policy
4 Points	• Quality policy regularly reviewed and revised
	• Achievement of quality policy objectives a high priority in overall performance reviews

Note: Each score assumes requirements of lower scores were also fulfilled

Figure 6-3. *Step 6 example.*

Category 1: Management behavior

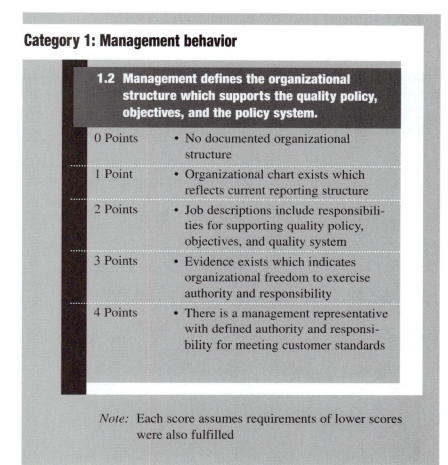

1.2 Management defines the organizational structure which supports the quality policy, objectives, and the policy system.

0 Points	• No documented organizational structure
1 Point	• Organizational chart exists which reflects current reporting structure
2 Points	• Job descriptions include responsibilities for supporting quality policy, objectives, and quality system
3 Points	• Evidence exists which indicates organizational freedom to exercise authority and responsibility
4 Points	• There is a management representative with defined authority and responsibility for meeting customer standards

Note: Each score assumes requirements of lower scores were also fulfilled

Figure 6-3. *Step 6 example (continued).*

Category 1: Management behavior

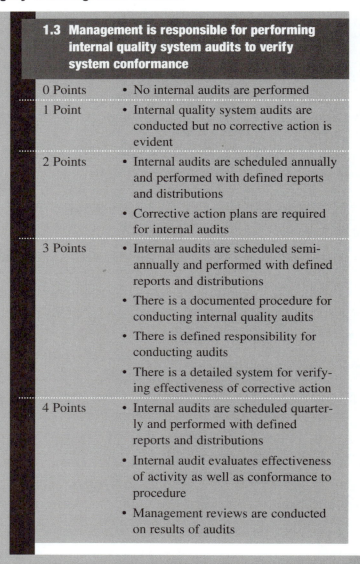

1.3 Management is responsible for performing internal quality system audits to verify system conformance

0 Points	• No internal audits are performed
1 Point	• Internal quality system audits are conducted but no corrective action is evident
2 Points	• Internal audits are scheduled annually and performed with defined reports and distributions • Corrective action plans are required for internal audits
3 Points	• Internal audits are scheduled semi-annually and performed with defined reports and distributions • There is a documented procedure for conducting internal quality audits • There is defined responsibility for conducting audits • There is a detailed system for verifying effectiveness of corrective action
4 Points	• Internal audits are scheduled quarterly and performed with defined reports and distributions • Internal audit evaluates effectiveness of activity as well as conformance to procedure • Management reviews are conducted on results of audits

Note: Each score assumes requirements of lower scores were also fulfilled

Figure 6-3. *Step 6 example (continued).*

Category 1: Management behavior

1.4 Management establishes and provides all personnel with necessary operational and quality training	
0 Points	• No formal training provided to employees
1 Point	• There is documented evidence that training is provided to all employees for operational procedures only • Training program addresses development of basic skills required for special processes
2 Points	• Evidence exists for training all levels of the organization in quality skill techniques and philosophies • There are records, by individual, that indicate type and extent of training
3 Points	• There is a documented procedure for evaluating ongoing training needs • There is a system in place which verifies effectiveness of training • A training plan is available which addresses future training requirements • The training program addresses development of special skills required for special processes
4 Points	• Annual training plans are addressed in budget requirements • Training program provides for qualification of personnel.

Note: Each score assumes requirements of lower scores were also fulfilled

Figure 6-3. *Step 6 example (continued).*

Assessment report card

	Category Description	Max. Score
1	Management Behavior	15
2	Quality Practices	12
3	Procurement	10
4	Materials	10
5	Manufacturing	20
6	Design Information	10
7	Statistical Techniques	15
8	Calibration	8
	Maximum Score	100

Final Score:

(Total Score ÷ Maximum Score) X 100

⬜ Excellent (90 to 100)   ⬜ Good (80 to 89)

⬜ Acceptable (70 to 79)   ⬜ Poor (less than 70)

Figure 6-3. *Step 6 example (continued).*

Educating Your Suppliers: The Supplier Symposium

" Leadership and learning are indispensable to each other. *"*

President John F. Kennedy

Motorola isn't the only big company *with its own "university" to upgrade the skills of its employees. Few, however, are as ambitious as Motorola U. about educating suppliers, too. In fact, Motorola has declared a number of courses mandatory for suppliers. These include design for manufacturing, design for assembly, cycle time, and statistical process control. Motorola U. was founded in the late 1970s with a five-year initiative to upgrade the skills of all employees. The company soon realized that educating suppliers only made sense, given their contribution to Motorola's aggressive quality targets. Noted Ken Stork, former corporate director of materials and purchasing, "We want our suppliers to learn what Motorola has already learned." So far, more than three-quarters of Motorola's preferred suppliers have enrolled.*

Xerox is another company with an extraordinary commitment to educating its suppliers, spending $500,000 annually on supplier training. It's paid off. Xerox owns the distinction of being the only Malcolm Baldrige National Quality Award winner that has had a supplier, Ames Rubber, win the award also. Think there could be a connection?

One of the best ways to cement your new relationship with selected suppliers is with a supplier symposium. This half-day or full-day meeting is your opportunity to get representatives from both companies in a room together to discuss Supply Chain Management. It also demonstrates that your company takes SCM seriously and that you want the suppliers to be just as committed. For that reason, keep the focus on work. This is not the time to schedule a golf outing or a trip to see a ball game.

Whatever you do, **don't** simply inform your suppliers via a letter or a phone call that they've been selected for your SCM program and leave it at that. Remember, you're inaugurating a process that will revolutionize the way you do business. You want to establish long-term, mutually beneficial relationships. The whole process can have great ramifications for the way you and your suppliers work together. It's just as important to win converts among your suppliers as it is within your own company. The way you inform your suppliers about SCM is a strong reflection of how your company feels about it, too.

Who To Invite to Your Symposium

Send invitations to the top three to six people at your supplier's facility. If they want to send a representative from the corporate office, that's fine, but you're more interested in the people with whom you'll actually be doing business. Make sure your company's counterparts of the supplier's representatives are included. Invitees should include:

- Top executive at the plant (president, CEO, owner, etc.)
- Vice president or director of operations and/or manufacturing
- Top quality person at the plant
- Top design engineer
- Top purchasing or materials person (if they have purchasing responsibility)
- The sales representative

Setting the Tone

Your top executive should kick off the meeting with a short welcome talk about where your company is going. His or her goal should be to set a positive tone, not to discuss SCM in any depth. This is a good opportunity to mention partnerships and the opportunities ahead for both companies. The supply chain team can get into the real meat of explaining SCM. It's important to keep the symposium upbeat and to stress the benefits to both companies. All of the people who speak for your company should discuss quality improvement, cost reduction, on-time delivery, and other benefits of Supply Chain Management.

Promote your program by example. Don't just tell your suppliers what you expect from them. Your suppliers will be skeptical and will see right through it if you're forcing a program on them to which you don't adhere yourself. It's important that you discuss your own company's experiences with Supply Chain Management. For example, you can talk about being a supplier to a customer that practices SCM. Speakers from various departments can talk about their own quality and productivity improvement initiatives, such as ISO 9000/QS 9000, SPC, Total Quality Management, or ERP.

Sample Agenda:

- Welcome and meet supplier's representatives
    1. Your management sets the tone by discussing your facility's continuous value improvement programs
- Outline the Supply Chain Management process
    1. The selection process
    2. Rating systems and report cards
    3. Assessment questionnaire
- Review corrective action form
- Identify responsibilities
- Identify benefits

- Tour of your plant: spend the most time in the areas where the supplier's products go into your process
- Obtain a simple customer-supplier agreement (see exercise).

Step 7 EXERCISE
Creating a Supply Chain Agreement

The Supply Chain Agreement simply provides an opportunity for suppliers to align themselves with your initiative. Both companies make a commitment. Few suppliers will sign it if they don't intend to participate. Do not try to turn the agreement into a complex legal document. If the lawyers on either side won't allow a written agreement, let it go. Make a handshake agreement with the people with whom you'll be dealing. For this exercise, create a simple document stating what you would like your Supply Chain Management process to accomplish for your company and for your suppliers. Here's an example:

The supply chain agreement

Acme's Responsibilities (Your Company)	Beta's Responsibilities (Supplier)
Provide clear standards for quality	Provide a capable process
Open and honest communication	Open and honest communication
Commit to continuous improvement	Commit to continuous improvement
Pay a fair price	Share cost savings
Evergreen contracts	Timely response to change

Acme Manufacturing (your company) is committed to a Supply Chain Management program with a continuous improvement philosophy.

Beta Widget Supply (the supplier) is committed to a Supply Chain Management program with a continuous improvement philosophy.

Signed:

_____   _____
Acme Representative   Beta Representative

Date: _____   Date: _____

Figure 7-1. *Put your agreement in writing.*

Obtaining 100% Agreement on Specifications

" Without a standard there is no logical basis for making a decision or taking **"** action.

Dr. Joseph M. Juran

Quality begins with design. *Too often we think of quality as a finished product or the ability to meet specifications. In reality, quality is a process and the process is only as good as its design. In an article in* Purchasing Magazine, *Bart Huthwaite, founder and director of the Institute for Competitive Design, noted that, "The real impact of a product's design on its manufacturing competitiveness must not be measured in direct dollar costs but how this key function influences 'manufacturability' of the product. A product's design ultimately determines whether it can be manufactured efficiently; if you don't get it right at the design stage, you will never get it right later, no matter how much automation, advanced technology, or SPC is used on the factory floor." This is an important lesson for your SCM team to keep in mind.*

Arriving at an across-the-board agreement (Figure 8-1) on component specifications may seem like a minor cog in the larger Supply Chain Management process. It's not! Lack of spec agreement has probably caused more problems between purchaser and supplier than any other single element. Obtaining 100% agreement within your company and with the supplier on part specifications is one of the keys to successful SCM.

Who Must Agree

Obviously, if your company is in aerospace, pharmaceuticals, or medical devices, your specification demands are going to be more stringent than if you're making garden tools. Even for shovels and rakes, how-

Quality begins with design specs

Department	New Role
Engineering	Provide specifications for parts that can be produced at a precise cost
Purchasing	Determine if the supply base can meet those specifications
Quality	Ensure that the incoming material meets the spec
Manufacturing	Produce the necessary yield if the supplier's product meets the specifications

Figure 8-1. *100% agreement on specifications is the first link in the quality chain.*

ever, you must have spec agreement.

Unfortunately, the traditional price-based, competitive bid process is ripe for spec problems. Trouble often arises when the design engineering department specs out a design in a vacuum, with no input from either purchasing or the supplier community. Purchasing is presented with a set of specifications that are set in stone. When a bid request is tossed to a hungry pack of competing suppliers, we all know the sentiment that prevails: "Win the bid first, worry about the details later." It's only after the bid is awarded and production begins that it becomes evident that the specifications cannot be met. Sometimes the spec is simply beyond industry tolerances. Unfortunately, at this point both purchaser and supplier are locked into a very sticky situation.

Spec Agreement First, then Price

The only way you can arrive at agreement on parts is to involve everyone who will have a hand in making and using them. Fortunately, the SCM team you've already assembled is just the group you need. One of your SCM team's roles will be to arrive at agreed-upon part specification before going out to bid. The first place to check your specifications is against standard industry tolerances. If your expectations exceed industry standards, you're already skating on thin ice.

As your Supply Chain Management program matures, you'll involve your suppliers in spec agreement, too. After all, if you've done your homework, the suppliers you've selected are experts. The sooner they're involved in the process, the smoother it will be for everyone.

The Penalty for Unrealistic Specs

As mentioned earlier, engineers are often very reluctant to allow suppliers input on design specs. Requests for loosened tolerances, in particular, are viewed in a dim light. Setting tolerances that cannot be met, however, only leads to waivers. In a Supply Chain Management environment, waivers are unacceptable. You must adopt the philosophy that products meet (reasonable) specifications or they will be rejected.

Waivers will simply tell your own employees, as well as your suppliers, that quality is a myth.

Production tolerances should be based on "best-in-industry" capability. Trying to advance the production mode technology beyond the industry's capabilities is a prescription for failure. Part of the problem can lie with engineers who have been cloistered for too long. They may have little understanding about your company's manufacturing processes, let alone the capabilities of your suppliers and the industry at large.

Part of your team's job is to tear down the internal silos and enable the company to function as a single organism. There must be 100% agreement that the specifications provided to the supplier will: produce a quality product, generate a product that can be inspected and tested against the specifications, provide the required yields in your process, and meet the conditions of your warranty to your customers. When a company reaches consensus on these issues and demonstrates SCM success, the engineering department, along with manufacturing, purchasing and quality—the "core four"—will join the team.

Step 8 EXERCISE
The Cost of Specification Disagreement

For this exercise, delve into the history of one of your company's parts that you know has had specification problems. Try to ascertain what they cost your company. If you're able to follow an actual paper trail of purchase orders, change orders, and price markups, so much the better. But even informally, in discussions with those involved, you'll be able to get an idea of the time, trouble, and expense that poor specs cost your company. Just as importantly, that's time, trouble, and expense that you'll be able to save your company in the future. If you discover that your company in fact does achieve 100% spec agreement before ordering, congratulations!

Performing a Tactical Supply Chain Assessment

" Take nothing on its looks; take everything on evidence. There's no better rule. *"*

Charles Dickens
Great Expectations

Motorola began a comprehensive assessment *of its own processes in the early 1980s. Called the quality system review, or QSR, the assessment enables each division to identify its strengths and to determine where it needs to improve. The division's general manager submits a "get well plan" upon completing the review. Before long, Motorola saw the value of prescribing the quality system review for its suppliers. As described in* Purchasing Magazine*:*

"In 1989, Motorola extended these QSRs to key suppliers and roughly 500 suppliers have undergone a QSR audit to date. These audits generally take about a week and are conducted by a cross-functional team led by the commodity manager. Like Motorola's own divisions, suppliers are required to submit a corrective action plan for any areas rated less than 'qualified.' Guidelines for scoring are fully explained in a handbook published by Motorola, enabling the supplier to do a self audit. In fact, suppliers are asked to do self-audits prior to meeting with the Motorola team."

I n Step 6, you began developing your tactical supply chain assessment. Now it's time to put it to use. A supplier assessment is performed by a team from your company. The assessment process itself may take several days. Remember, you won't be going to your supplier's facility just for a visit—you're going to gather specific information that's truly relevant to your company's ability to compete.

Your Supplier Assessment Team

Your best guarantee of a good, useful assessment is a savvy cross-functional team to administer it. There are several reasons why an audit should be performed by a team and not by just one or two people. Most importantly, a team will enable you to bring the maximum amount of expertise to your assessments. Logistically, you'll also be gathering more information than a single person can realistically gather. Finally, any one person will want to stay in his or her "comfort zone." We're only human. A person from your purchasing department will not feel comfortable trying to evaluate manufacturing systems with which he or she has little experience. Nor will that person's evaluation be very knowledgeable. Instead, a purchaser will be most comfortable—and most effective—evaluating procurement, receiving, and inventory management.

Your assessment team may or may not include members of your supply chain management team. That's not important, as long as they understand their tasks. Ideally, your team will include individuals qualified to evaluate each of the areas you're assessing. We suggest that your team include at least one person from each of the following areas:

- Purchasing
- Manufacturing
- Engineering
- Quality

In addition, select a team that can stay together for a full series of assessments, such as assessments of all the suppliers in a specific commodity family. There are several benefits to establishing a permanent or semi-permanent assessment team: You'll be ensured of consistent scoring; your team will become more knowledgeable about the assessment process; and, as they visit a number of supplier sites, team members will capture valuable information about your entire base of suppliers.

Naturally, the number of people on your assessment team will depend on management's commitment to your assessment program. Also, the aggressiveness of your assessment schedule and the amount of time needed away from the office will affect who's on your team. That's why it's important to plan your assessment program carefully. It's better to underestimate how much you can get done than to bite off more than you can chew.

Invariably, during an assessment your SCM team will learn ways to improve the processes in your facility to make life better for the supplier. We've had experience doing hundreds of assessments and that's always been the case. **Learning is not a one-way street**.

Performing Your Assessment

When you send a team out to a supplier's facility to perform an audit, the goal is not to complete a checklist and return home as quickly as possible. On the contrary, the team must have time to perform an in-depth assessment. One day is not enough. Two days may be enough time, but only if you have a team of adequate size. Remember, your company could be spending hundreds of thousands, perhaps millions, of dollars with a supplier. You're also looking for suppliers with whom you can establish a long-term relationship. This is your opportunity to acquire information that will enable that relationship to thrive and grow, for the benefit of your company, your supplier, and your customers. One-day assessments are little more than auditing the paper trail.

Before You Go

Have your assessment tool ready well before the audit and ensure that team members know how to use it. Make sure the supplier's management knows your team is coming and why. Set firm dates and times for your assessment and stick to them. Ensure that every department with which you will be dealing has been notified that they'll be assessed, understands why, and will give your team full cooperation. If you'll need access to records or information that aren't readily available, such as SPC history or procurement records, request in advance that they be available. If any areas will be off-limits to your assessment team, determine them in advance. Once the assessment is in progress, you won't want to waste time on misunderstandings or problems over access.

This will be a good time to reiterate to the supplier the purpose of the assessment and to reassure the supplier that it's a critical part of your commitment to a long-term, mutually beneficial relationship.

Finally, before you arrive at the facility, your team should be briefed on individual assignments and timetables. The time spent on any one element of your assessment will depend on its importance to your company. In Figure 9-1, you can see that weights have been assigned to each element. The areas assigned the most weight are the most important. That's where your team will spend the most time.

At the Supplier's Facility

Once your team is on site, have the members meet with the heads of the departments they'll be evaluating, as well as anyone in the department from whom they'll need cooperation. If the supplier's management requests that the assessment be explained or discussed at a management meeting, do it prior to the actual assessment. Otherwise, make sure it happens first thing in the morning. You won't want your team members twiddling their thumbs while a meeting drags through a lengthy agenda.

Team members should again convey to department heads exactly what they'll be doing and what their requirements will be. Your team members should take the lead in establishing a spirit of cordiality and cooperation. Although your company is the buyer, and in theory holds the power of the purse, remember that the assessment will further the aim of establishing a long-term, win-win relationship. Arrogance or rudeness on the part of your assessment team will do little to reassure the supplier of your company's commitment to such a relationship.

Depending upon the department, the assessment will cause some disruption of the supplier's normal routine. Team members should be sensitive about keeping interruptions to a minimum. However, the primary goal of your team will be to gather information. Some break in normal routine will be inevitable.

It's a good idea for your assessment team members to meet and debrief at the end of each day. Any unforeseen difficulties can be discussed. Your team leader should be ready to contact supplier management, or your own senior management, if difficulties arise that require intervention.

Scoring Your Suppliers

As in other parts of our supply chain management process, we recommend using a weighted average to score your assessment. Weighting ensures that the areas of most importance to your company will contribute most to the score.

Figure 9-1 shows a hypothetical scoring report based on the eight elements discussed in Step 6. In this example, the elements are weighted from 8% to 20%. Management behavior and statistical process control are weighted at 20%. You'll determine the weights according to your company's priorities. However, the weights in the example add up to 100%. We encourage you to shoot for totals of 100 or 1,000 to keep the scoring simple. Information that can be understood at a glance is all the more valuable.

The figures in the "Score" column are simple totals carried over from the assessment report. Multiplying the score by the weight gives you the "Total," or weighted score. Adding the figures in the Total column, gives the supplier's score. In the example, the score is 72.15.

What the Assessment Scores Tell You

From the scores, you can identify the areas in the supplier company that most need improvement. By comparing the internal assessment to the report card on the same supplier, you can begin to get at the root of problems. For example, if your report cards on Supplier C show a high rate of rework on a particular part, and your assessment reveals that

Supplier assessment report

Supplier: ABC Company

Elements	Weight	Score	Total
1 Management Behavior	15%	75	11.25*
2 Quality Practices	12%	85	10.2
3 Procurement	10%	60	6.0
4 Materials	10%	80	8.0
5 Manufacturing	20%	60	12.0
6 Design Information	10%	40	4.0
7 Statistical Techniques	15%	90	13.5
8 Calibration	8%	90	7.2
Totals	100%		72.15

*.15 X 75 = 11.25

Figure 9-1. *Determine the weights according to your company's priorities.*

Supplier C has no formal procedures for the control and calibration of test equipment, then you may have identified the problem. This gives you the opportunity to work with the supplier on bringing calibration standards up to your company's expectations. In other words, rather than absorbing the cost of rework, losing time for re-shipment, or searching for a new supplier, you can solve the problem. The result will be a lower cost for you and the supplier. In addition, you will have taken a positive step forward in your relationship with your supplier.

Assessment scores will also enable you to compare suppliers. You can find many uses for comparative information. For example, if you're looking for a supplier who can supply a sub-assembly with tighter than usual design tolerances, you can tell at a glance which supplier has the best record for quality, calibration, and SPC.

Finally, assessment scores will give you the opportunity to set a target that you expect the supplier to achieve on the next assessment. For example, you can tell a supplier who scores 75 on one element of the assessment that you expect a score of 85 on the next visit. This is in keeping with the philosophy of continuous improvement.

Alternatives to an Assessment

There's absolutely no question of the value of supplier assessments. However, they are also time consuming and costly. Once you've assessed your top tier of suppliers, you may not be able to justify the time and expense of a full team assessment for smaller accounts. In fact, they may not be necessary. Alternatives include accepting an ISO 9000 or QSO 9000 report or a third-party assessment done by another company that does business with that supplier.

You can also have the supplier do a self-assessment using your forms. (For small companies, you may want to shorten the form, too.) Naturally, it won't be as reliable as an assessment performed by your team. However, in self-administering the assessment, the supplier will be learning your standards. Moreover, the assessment form will provide a quality target for the supplier.

Some fudging of the numbers can be expected on a self-assessment. This can be minimized by leaving open the possibility of a "live" assessment in the future. Compare self-assessments to supplier report cards. You will very rarely find a company that scores poorly at your back door but comes through an assessment with flying colors. If the two reports contradict each other, investigate further.

Assessing Distributors

If your company is being supplied by a distributor, you should still do an assessment, with some changes. You won't assess a distributor on its manufacturing capabilities, for instance. However, a distributor must still be held accountable for manufacturing results, such as quality, even if the fault lies with the manufacturer. You can assist the distributor by making sure the manufacturer gets the message that its poor performance is going to cost the distributor—and therefore the manufacturer—your business.

When To Stop Doing Assessments

When a supplier shows excellent results on six or seven assessments, you know they have a legitimately high-quality operation dedicated to continuous improvement. At that point, you can elect to stop doing assessments entirely or cut down to a schedule of once every two or three years. Remember, the goal is to streamline. Ultimately, assessments should reduce work, not add to it.

When the assessments no longer have value in your eyes or in the eyes of your suppliers, we recommend that you consider replacing them with process improvement studies.

Final Words on Maximizing the Benefits of an Assessment

- Send your suppliers your assessment tool and have them perform a self-assessment about 30 days before your assessment team arrives.
- Make sure your products are on the supplier's production line during your assessment.
- The assessment tool must eliminate subjectivity. This can be done by careful formulation of each assessment question, particularly with regard to identifying what the supplier must do to earn the maximum points. See the examples in Step 6.

Step 9 EXERCISE
Testing Your Assessment Tool

As mentioned in Step 6, the best practice for performing a supply chain audit is to perform a pilot test with your assessment tool. Use it to evaluate a department or division in your company. The goal of the test is to see how well the assessment tool works and to allow time for modification and fine tuning. Look for sections with too much ambiguity in the scoring and others that can be simplified without compromising your ability to collect useful information. A test also gives your assessment team an opportunity to become familiar with using the form.

Evaluating Bids Using Supply Chain Performance Indexes

" There is hardly anything in this world that someone can't make a little worse and sell a little cheaper. People who consider price alone are this person's lawful prey. *"*

Sun Microsystems Inc., *the network-computing giant, faces a harsh reality: The workstations they produce have an average life-cycle of about 12 months. With a never-ending stream of new products, Sun depends heavily on a cadre of nimble, responsive suppliers. Time-to-market is the company's rallying cry. Quality, delivery, and lead time are more than just idle concepts; if Sun's suppliers fall down in any of these areas, the company is brought to its knees.*

One way Sun evaluates its suppliers is through "scorecards" that yield performance indexes. By looking at non-productive events, the scorecards rate the total cost of ownership (TCOO in Sun shorthand). The scorecards compare suppliers within commodity groups and also measure performance against Sun's standards.

Sun collects data in five performance areas: price, quality, delivery, technology, and service. Using the scorecards, the company generates indexes which help them assess the true price of a supplier's bid. A theoretically perfect rating equals 1. Non-conformance items raise the index above 1. For example, a performance index of 1.3 means that Sun spends an additional 30 cents for each dollar it pays to that supplier. To determine the supplier's actual cost, Sun would multiply their bid by the index factor of 1.3. During a recent quarterly review, the company issued 35 scorecards that ranged from a top performing index of 1.07 down to 1.67.

Sun shares performance indexes with its suppliers on a regular basis. It also brings in upper management from its 20 largest suppliers twice a year for a scorecard presentation. In this way, Sun keeps a continuous improvement mentality on the front burner.

I f your company has followed the program outlined in this book thus far, you are surely committed to the principles and practices of Supply Chain Management. You are reconfiguring the traditional customer-supplier relationship and are forging new partnerships. In doing so, you're fundamentally changing the perceptions and attitudes of those within your company towards suppliers. You've established an SCM team that is leading your company through this wholesale cultural change. You're paring down the number of suppliers and carefully evaluating those that remain. You are generating supplier report cards and sharing this information throughout your company. Everything is humming along according to plan.

So, now it's time for your company to send out quotes. You collect the bids and present them to senior management. Armed with all of the SCM data you've judiciously collected, senior management carefully considers the bids and awards the contract...*based on price.*

In that defining moment, all of SCM's precepts are suddenly meaningless. All of the talk about awarding business based on report card performance is hollow. Your suppliers confirm their skeptical suspicions and it's back to business as usual.

How can things go so terribly wrong when it's SCM gut-check time and real dollars are on the line? It's human nature. It's difficult to act against instinct. Senior management looks at your suppliers' bids and their *minds* race as they ponder intangibles such as delivery, quality and value. But, when they look at unit prices, their *hearts* prevail and SCM concepts go out the window.

We call it the $16 light bulb dilemma. We've all been faced with this predicament. You need to replace a light bulb and you've depleted the stash in your utility closet. You head off to the hardware store and stare at the items on the shelf. Do you stick with a tried-and-true 99¢ incandescent bulb or do you make the switch to a $16 compact fluorescent bulb? It's gut-check time. Your mind says the fluorescent bulb will produce comparable light, last much longer, and use much less electricity over the life of the product. In the long run, you'll end up saving money. You start to consider the extra space you'll gain in your utility closet when you no longer have to keep a supply of bulbs on hand. You also think about the time you'll save on trips to the hardware store and changing bulbs. By using less energy, the compact fluorescent bulbs are even better for the environment, you tell yourself.

But the lure of the 99¢ light bulb is intoxicating. No matter how you try to rationalize it, *it just doesn't feel right* to pay an extra $15.01 for the other light bulb. With limited cash on hand, your good sense is dashed. Another casualty of "purchasing mindset," you sheepishly pick up the $3.96 incandescent bulb four-pack and head off to the cash register.

But wait! What if the hardware store printed the **total cost** of the two light bulbs in big, bold numbers next to their prices on the shelf signs? What if the bulbs' life-cycle costs like electricity use, number of replacements, transportation, and installation labor were factored in? How would you respond if the total cost of the incandescent light bulb, say $38, was plainly listed on the hardware store shelf next to the fluorescent bulb's projected total cost of $21?

This is the theory behind performance indexes. We take "soft" information like quality and on-time delivery that we can grasp intellectually and convert it to "hard" numbers that we can embrace intuitively. Performance indexes measure the sometimes elusive concept of **value**. If your SCM team is able to present your suppliers' total bottom-line impact on your company, even senior management will be able to relate to the concept and make informed purchasing decisions.

There are two types of performance indexes we will explore in this chapter. The first kind, **supplier rating indexes**, are intended for companies with young SCM programs. Even with limited performance history data, your team will be able to make preliminary comparisons of your suppliers using these indexes. Later in the chapter, we will look at different types of **supplier performance indexes** that more mature programs can generate.

Start with Supplier Rating Indexes

For most companies, purchasing decisions are made by the time-honored traditions of either requesting bids and praying or paying low and suffering. Performance indexes will help your company move away from these baseless models and toward one in which you'll have a better sense of what you're really getting for your purchasing dollars. You'll be able to translate your suppliers' bids into total cost ratings. The more information you're able to capture—floor failures, rework labor, material delivered short, etc.—the more sophisticated your indexes will be.

Most new SCM programs, however, simply don't have the infrastructure in place to gather lots of data. Supplier rating indexes will allow your company to make meaningful cost comparisons with minimal information. Since you will need some history to generate data however, supplier rating indexes cannot be used with new suppliers. For each supplier providing a bid, you'll calculate a comparative rate with 100 as a perfect score. The closer to 100, the better overall value the bid represents, regardless of price.

Weighing Price

For supplier rating index elements, use categories that are relevant to your industry. Most companies will want to return to the familiar elements of quality, delivery, and price. As Figure 10-1 illustrates, however, because we're scrutinizing bids, price plays a more significant role here than it does in the SCM report cards and other examples we looked at earlier in the book. In this typical hypothetical case, we've assigned a relative weight of 50 for price while quality and delivery receive 30 and 20 points, respectively.

To determine the price component of the supplier rating index, first gather all of the bids together for the product you want to award to one of your suppliers. In the example cited in Figure 10-2, three suppliers have submitted bids with unit prices ranging from $120 to $140. Make sure that the specifications are identical for each of the bids so that you're comparing like bid prices.

Use the lowest bid (in this case, $120) as the base price. Enter the base price in the numerator and each of the bid prices in the denominator, then divide to determine the weight factor for each bid. Multiply each weight factor by the total number of possible price points (in this case, 50) to determine each supplier's price rating. Because supplier A in Figure 10-2 offered the lowest price, that supplier receives the full 50 points.

Sample supplier rating index elements and weights

Element	Points
Price	50
Quality	30
Delivery	20
Total points	100

Figure 10-1. *Price moves to a more prominent position for supplier rating indexes.*

Calculating the price component of a supplier rating index

Supplier	Bid Price		Bid Ratio		Weight Factor		Available Points		Price Rating
A	$120	=	120/120	=	1	X	50	=	50
B	$130	=	120/130	=	.923	X	50	=	46.2
C	$140	=	120/140	=	.828	X	50	=	41.4

Figure 10-2. *Use the lowest bid in the numerator of the bid ratio and divide to determine the weight factor.*

Calculating the quality component of a supplier rating index

Supplier	Shipments Received		Shipments Accepted		Weight Factor		Available Points		Quality Rating
A	50	÷	46	=	.92	X	30	=	27.6
B	20	÷	20	=	1	X	30	=	30.0
C	30	÷	29	=	.967	X	30	=	29.0

Figure 10-3. *Divide the number of shipments accepted into the total shipments received to determine the weight factor.*

Convert Quality and Delivery to a Rating

To calculate a quality rating, use existing receiving inspection data for each of the suppliers. For a more accurate picture, you'll want to use as long a performance period as possible, up to the past twelve months. "Quality" here simply refers to the ratio of accepted shipments to total shipments received. You can add other criteria to help refine the quality rating as well as other components of the supplier rating index. But, this index is designed to be a broad overview and, in general, you'll want to keep things simple.

In the example listed in Figure 10-3, the number of shipments accepted divided into the total number of shipments received yields a weight factor for each bid. Multiply each weight factor by the number of possible quality points (in this case, 30) to determine each supplier's quality rating. Because the company accepted all shipments from supplier B in Figure 10-3, that supplier receives the full 30 points.

Use the number of on-time shipments to generate the delivery rating. Again, you could consider the relative weights of early deliveries and other more discrete delivery factors but the goal is to maintain simplicity. In Figure 10-4, the number of on-time shipments divided into the total number of shipments received yields a weight factor for each bid. Multiply each weight factor by the number of possible delivery points (in this case, 20) to determine each supplier's delivery rating.

As illustrated in Figure 10-5, add all of the component ratings together to calculate the overall supplier rating index. In this example, supplier B scored the highest. Although its price is higher than supplier A's, the significantly superior quality and delivery it offers more than offsets the price variance.

As supplier C demonstrates in Figure 10-5, the money you spend does not always equal the value received. Its higher bidding price was not offset by better quality or delivery. With supplier rating indexes, your company will be able to better determine the "best" quote without

Calculating the delivery component of a supplier rating index

Supplier	Shipments Received		On-Time Shipments		Weight Factor		Available Points		Delivery Rating
A	50	÷	39	=	.78	X	20	=	15.6
B	20	÷	18	=	.90	X	20	=	18
C	30	÷	24	=	.80	X	20	=	16

Figure 10-4. *Divide the number of on-time shipments into the total shipments received to determine the weight factor.*

Calculating the supplier rating index

Supplier	Price Rating		Quality Rating		Delivery Rating		Overall Rating
A	50.0	+	27.6	+	15.6	=	93.2
B	46.2	+	30.9	+	18.0	=	95.1
C	41.4	+	29.0	+	16.0	=	86.4

Figure 10-5. *Add the component ratings together to determine the overall rating index.*

focusing exclusively on price. You'll have the tools to extract the lowest total cost from a group of your suppliers' bids.

Looking at Life-Cycle Costs

For another way to examine quotes, consider the material's life-cycle costs. That is, when you to decide to accept a bid, what will be the actual costs to your company during the life of the product? That's what the light bulb analogy at the beginning of this chapter was all about.

You need to consider the long-term ramifications of your purchasing decision. For example, what internal modifications might you have to make to accommodate the purchased material? What happens when the part breaks down with one of your customers? What about any added costs you may have to incur, such as shipping, administration, and labor, to replace a failed part? Other life-cycle considerations include costs related to purchasing, receiving inspection costs, and costs associated with supplier problems.

The goal is to make purchasing decisions that minimize total costs. The problem is that no one department is responsible for minimizing life-cycle costs. Everybody has got a piece of the puzzle: Purchasing tries to minimize unit prices. Production tries to minimize labor costs. Field service tries to reduce their costs. It's the job of the SCM team to pull everything together and look at the big picture.

When companies take a broad view, they can see that quality, delivery, and other hidden factors do, indeed, cost real dollars. The true costs of materials reveal themselves—over time. That's why more sophisticated performance indexes, the subject of the next section in this chapter, are so important for successful SCM programs. They measure a supplier's comprehensive performance history and provide a more accurate means to evaluate quotes.

Incorporating Supplier Performance Indexes

SCM teams generate performance indexes by incorporating as many failure costs associated with a supplier as possible. It can take considerable effort for a company to calculate and capture the cost impact of scrap, floor failures, early deliveries, and other failure costs. That's why young SCM programs don't generally adopt performance indexes right away. But they are a vital function and a critical goal for your SCM team.

There are five types of supplier performance indexes:

- **Part performance index**
- **Commodity performance index**
- **Supplier performance index**
- **Quality performance index**
- **Delivery performance index**

Most companies focus on one of the first three indexes since they also incorporate quality and delivery information. Because so much data is involved, few SCM teams use more than one index when reviewing a bid. Companies that have automated the data capturing process and have their MIS departments actively involved are an exception; they can easily generate multiple performance indexes and evaluate bids from different perspectives.

As Figure 10-6 shows, the formula to determine performance indexes is quite simple. Add non-productive costs to purchased costs and divide by the purchased costs. If, for example, you purchased a part that cost, in aggregate, $10,000 over a 12-month period and incurred $1500 of non-productive costs for that part, you would add $10,000 and $1500, then divide by $10,000 to yield a supply performance index of 1.15.

To calculate the five different kinds of performance indexes, the formula remains the same but the variables change.

Part performance index (PPI): As its name implies, a PPI focuses on the costs associated with an individual part from a supplier. It is used

DATA DILEMMA

Failure rates, corrective action reports, excess material costs: How could any company gather all this information? We know that many of you are thinking you don't have the people or the time to tackle these labor-intensive tasks. Yet, you have plenty of time to put out the daily fires caused by supplier failures under traditional supply management models. Remember, this is a new approach. SCM is designed to bring down costs, improve efficiencies, and reduce wasted time.

If you're thinking that much of the prescribed recordkeeping for Supply Chain Management falls into the "easier said than done" category, we have a word for you: automation. The sooner you can automate data capturing, the sooner you can generate comprehensive reports at the mere touch of a button.

The best SCM programs automate the process at every step. Using computer systems, employees from the loading dock, inspection, assembly, shipping, and everywhere along the line track supplies and log all relevant information. Once the system is in place, it's quick and painless to maintain. Your MIS department can be a key ally in establishing and administering data collection.

You may want to consider software packages such as Rohby's Supplier Analysis Systems (410-715-0628). It maintains non-conformance costs and produces Supplier Report Cards and Indexes. The software is PC-based (Windows) and extremely user friendly.

For additional information about cost-of-quality tracking programs, contact the American Society for Quality (ASQ) at 800-248-1946.

during bid evaluations to identify the lowest total cost.

Commodity performance index (CPI): For a large company that deals in thousands of parts, maintaining individual performance indexes for each part can be unwieldy. That's why many companies use commodity performance indexes instead. CPIs use cost data from a supplier's commodity group. If a commodity such as electronics is too broad, you may want to consider narrowing the grouping to a family of parts such as circuits, power supplies, or resistors. Like PPIs, companies use CPIs during the bid evaluations to identify the lowest total cost. Companies also used CPIs to determine total costs when they buy a "new" part which they have never purchased but for which the supplier in that commodity has expertise.

Supplier performance index (SPI): This index examines the costs associated with everything purchased from a supplier. We advise companies to use SPIs only when all the parts you purchase from a supplier are comparable in price. If some items cost a few dollars and you experience a problem with an item that costs a few hundred dollars, that could unfairly skew the SPI results for that supplier. Companies mainly use this index to track supplier trends.

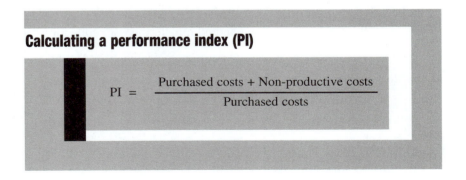

Calculating a performance index (PI)

$$PI = \frac{\text{Purchased costs} + \text{Non-productive costs}}{\text{Purchased costs}}$$

Figure 10-6. *Add purchased costs to non-productive costs and divide by purchased costs to determine a performance index.*

Quality performance index (QPI); delivery performance index (DPI): Part, commodity, and supplier indexes monitor all non-productive costs, including quality and delivery. Quality and delivery performance indexes, however, only focus on quality or delivery data.

When MIS is involved and you have the automated ability to easily capture data and generate reports, use quality and delivery indexes along with all of the first three indexes (PPI, CPI and SPI). Otherwise, you'll probably want to forego QPI and DPI and stick with one of the first three indexes.

When you need to calculate a performance index, you should be able to readily obtain purchased costs, the amount of money you have spent with a supplier for a part or commodity, through accounts payable or purchasing systems. You may want to add transportation costs to purchased costs for performance indexes. Often, any savings from lower unit costs are offset by increased freight costs.

Use Performance Indexes to Determine "Best Value" Price

As you can see, performance indexes will be some number greater than one. Hypothetically, a perfect index of one would indicate that your company has not incurred any non-productive costs for that part, commodity, or supplier. In the real world, this is highly unlikely. The closer to one, the better the performance index.

To calculate the "best value" price among a group of bids, multiply the quoted price by the performance index, as shown in Figure 10-7. As demonstrated, the lowest purchase price will not normally match the "best value" price. By factoring in non-productive costs, supplier C in this example ends up with a considerably better total cost even though its quoted unit price falls in the middle.

Capturing Non-Productive Costs

Non-productive costs include any costs that are outside of the norm for the part, commodity, or supplier you are evaluating. You'll want to gather as comprehensive a list as possible. In most cases, you'll need to convert the amount of time your company spends dealing with non-conformance elements into dollars. One of the easiest ways to do this is to calculate the average person-hours for each failure occurrence and maintain a record of the occurrences. On a monthly basis, multiply the number of occurrences by the average person-hours for each occurrence to establish the amount of time spent responding to each failure item. Then multiply that number by the average person-hour cost at your company to establish the dollar cost impact of each failure. This process is illustrated in Figure 10-10 later in this chapter.

Some non-productive costs might include costs associated with:
- Rejection of non-conforming material at the supplier
- Rejection of non-conforming material at your facility
- Acceptance of non-conforming material
- Reworking of non-conforming materials
- Floor failures
- Material delivered late or early
- Material delivered short or over
- Warranty costs due to supplier problems

Calculating the "best value" price

Supplier	Quoted Price		PPI		Total Costs
A	$2000	X	1.35	=	$2700
B	$2100	X	1.25	=	$2625
C	$2050	X	1.10	=	$2255

Figure 10-7. *Consider non-productive costs. Multiply the performance index by the quoted price to determine the best value.*

What if you want to determine a performance index for a new supplier and have no history of non-productive costs upon which to draw? You can use a composite commodity index, taking an average of the indexes for suppliers that provide that commodity. It's not 100% accurate but it will give you a rough sense of the industry's capability and the likely performance of the new supplier.

There is a far better solution. As described in the preceding chapter, visit the new supplier's facility. Examine their processes. Inspect their records. Ask about back orders and yields. Can they really deliver what they say they can in their bid? Use this information in tandem with an industry average commodity index to more precisely evaluate a new supplier's bid.

To calculate a performance index, it is preferable, but not necessary, to incorporate as much failure cost data as possible. Figure 10-8 shows a monthly non-productive report that measures two failure categories: scrap cost and labor and overhead cost. At the company that prepared this report, every time a part needed to be scrapped or reworked, department personnel filled out a form to capture the information. The scrap costs refer to the purchase price for the parts that have been lost due to part failure. The labor and overhead covers the materials and person-hours required to rework or scrap the failed part.

In Figure 10-9, the cumulative scrap and labor and overhead failure costs are added together to produce a 12-month non-productive cost for each part. These non-productive costs, along with the parts' year-to-date purchase costs would be plugged into the performance index formula presented in Figure 10-6 to calculate the PPI. The non-conformance costs demonstrate how much additional money your company has to add to products in order to make them functional.

Let's examine a more advanced program that captures many different types of non-productive cost information. The company cited in Figure 10-10 is more automated and uses barcode data collection systems to record all of its data. The $50 per person-hour figure is a

Purchased material non-productive report

Month: November

Supplier	NC* Date	NC* Qty.	Part No.	Part Description	Defect Description	Status	Scrap Cost	Current L&O Cost
Cut-Rate, Inc.	11/14	22	64211	Electrical accessory	Missing threads	Scrap	$44.09	$11.49
	11/18	13	64211	Electrical accessory	Will not operate	Rework		$106.51
						Subtotal	$44.09	$118.00
Hometown QI	11/2	2	3640	Valve	Leaks	Rework		$46.76
	11/24	6	3650	Support bracket	Cracked	Scrap	$67.14	
						Subtotal	$67.14	$46.76
						TOTAL	$111.23	$164.76

*NC= Non-Conforming

Figure 10-8. *Sample monthly supplier non-productive cost report.*

composite of all of the hourly and salaried workers who interact with the parts being evaluated. The person-hours per occurrence is either the actual time captured by the barcode system or the average amount of time it takes people from the company to deal with the failure item. The dollar amounts listed in the table represent the cost impact to the company for each occurrence. They were calculated by multiplying the person-hours per occurrence by the average person-hour figure of $50. Hence, the cost to inspect a failed piece that was accepted with repair, estimated to take $3/10$ of an hour, is listed as $15.

The number of occurrences are tallied each month, multiplied by the cost per occurrence, and added together to yield a monthly total non-productive cost. The monthly total non-productive costs would then be added together on a revolving 12-month basis to generate a total non-productive cost. This is the number that would be inserted into the performance index formula presented in Figure 10-6.

Figure 10-11 shows a sample supplier performance index report card. The deficiencies refer to the number of non-productive cost occurrences reported for the period. The company includes an average

Purchased material non-productive overview report

Last 12 months: September, 1997 to September, 1998

Supplier	Part Number	L&O	Scrap	NC Cost
Precision AX	53211-6	$2050	$376	$2426
Hometown QI	3650	$1682	$233	$1915
Cut-Rate, Inc.	64211	$523	$310	$833

Figure 10-9. *Sample 12-month supplier non-productive cost report.*

Non-productive manufacturing costs

Supplier: XYZ Company

Function	Person-hours per Occurrence	Return to Supplier	Accept with Repair	Accept NC Material	Material Late	Material Early	Excess Material	Short Material
Receiving Inspection	.3			$15				
Material Review	.9	$45						
Technical Analysis	1.0		$50					
Material Disposition	.6	$30						
Production Reschedules	2.1				$105			
Rework	*		R					
Inspection	.3		$15					
Packaging	.4	$20						
Shipping Documentation	.2				$10			
Transportation	*	R						
Inventory/Carrying Cost	*						$60	

*Variable cost, dependent upon situation. Typical cost assumed when necessary.

R=Reimbursed by direct supplier charge.

Figure 10-10. Sample non-productive manufacturing costs. Costs are determined at $50 per person-hour.

commodity performance index and a best-of-industry index along with the supplier's performance index.

Integrate Performance Indexes into Your Comprehensive SCM Program

The goal with performance indexes is not to "catch" suppliers doing something wrong. Neither do you want to use performance indexes to justify hardball negotiations. The goal is to determine the real total cost of suppliers' bids when you request quotes.

You'll also want to freely share performance index information throughout your company—and with your suppliers. As part of SCM's

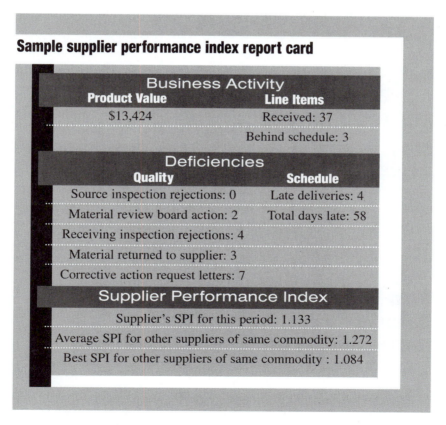

Figure 10-11. *Share your SPI report cards with your suppliers.*

commitment to open communication, letting your suppliers see the performance indexes you generate will benefit both your company and your suppliers. As shown in Figure 10-11, sharing SPI report cards, which state suppliers' SPIs, the average SPIs for other suppliers of the same commodities, and the best SPIs, acknowledges suppliers' efforts and gives them an incentive to improve their performance. And that contributes to the ultimate goal of Supply Chain Management: Mutually beneficial partnerships between you and your suppliers in which everyone strives for continual improvements.

Superior suppliers are not found, they are developed. You'll want to treat suppliers as an extension of your organization—even during the bidding process. Establish meaningful performance objectives, give suppliers an opportunity to excel and reward exceptional performance with new business. You and your suppliers will discover great rewards when you travel on the quality journey together.

Step 10 EXERCISES
Calculate a Performance Index
Determine the Best "Total Value" Bid

A. Using Figure 10-12, convert each of the person-hours per failure occurrence into dollar costs by multiplying by the per person-hour cost as shown in the receiving inspection example. Round to the nearest whole dollar.

Non-productive manufacturing costs

Supplier: **A**

Determine costs at $45 per person-hour

Function	Return to Supplier	Accept with Repair	Accept NC Material	Material Late	Material Early	Excess Material	Short Material
Receiving Inspection			.4= $18				
Material Review	1 =						
Technical Analysis		1.1=					
Material Disposition	.8=						
Production Reschedules				2=			
Rework		R					
Inspection		.3=					
Packaging	.5=			2=			
Shipping Documentation							
Transportation	R						
Inventory/Carrying Cost							

*Variable cost, dependent upon situation. Typical cost assumed when necessary.

R=Reimbursed by direct supplier charge.

Figure 10-12. *Determine non-productive manufacturing costs per occurrence.*

B. Using Figure 10-13, determine December's monthly purchased materials non-productive report for supplier A. As shown in the receiving inspection example, multiply the number of occurrences for each failure item by the cost per occurrence as calculated in Figure 10-12.

Monthly purchased materials non-productive report

Supplier: **A**

Function	Number of Occurrences	Cost per Occurrence	Total Cost
Receiving Inspection (accept non-conforming material)	6	$18	$108
Material Review (return to supplier)	3	$	$
Technical Analysis (accept with repair)	2	$	$
Material Disposition (return to supplier)	4	$	$
Production Reschedules	0	$	$
Rework	0	$	$
Inspection (accept with repair)	6	$	$
Packaging (return to supplier)	4	$	$
Shipping Documentation (material late)	7	$	$
Transportation	0	$	$
TOTALS	$		$

Figure 10-13. *Calculate monthly non-productive costs.*

C. Using Figure 10-14, add the monthly costs to determine the year-to-date non-productive costs for Supplier A. For the month of December, insert the total cost you calculated in Figure 10-13.

Year-to-date non-productive costs

Month	Monthly Non-Productive Costs
January	$457
February	$298
March	$784
April	$312
May	$569
June	$112
July	$434
August	$754
September	$205
October	$365
November	$115
December	$
Year-to-Date Total	$

Figure 10-14. *Determine the year-to-date non-productive costs.*

D. In Figure 10-15, use the formula from Figure 10-6 to calculate the
    performance indexes for each of the suppliers. For supplier A use
    the year-to-date total non productive costs you determined in
    Figure 10-14.

Determine supplier performance indexes

Supplier	YTD Purchased Costs	YTD Non-Productive Costs	Supplier Performance Index
A	$48,576	$	$
B	$23,687	$6012	$
C	$76,898	$5231	$

Figure 10-15. *Calculate the performance indexes.*

E. You have requested bids for a new part order. In Figure 10-16,
    determine the total evaluated costs. Insert the SPI performance
    indexes you calculated in Figure 10-15. Multiply the performance
    index by the quoted price to determine the best value. Which sup-
    plier offers the best value price?

Calculate the best value price

Supplier	Quoted Price		SPI		Total Evaluated Costs
A	$3300	X		=	$
B	$3200	X		=	$
C	$3600	X		=	$

Figure 10-16. *Compare price and value among suppliers.*

Keeping Your Suppliers on Track

" Two approaches to improvement to avoid: systems without passion and passion *"* without systems.

Tom Peters,
Thriving On Chaos

Caterpillar Inc. has one of the most proactive approaches *to promoting continuous improvement among its suppliers. The centerpiece of the effort is the Caterpillar Quality Institute. This "university without walls" offers a changing list of courses, seminars, and training sessions attuned to the needs of Caterpillar and its suppliers. The company views educating suppliers as a win for all involved. Quoted in* Purchasing Magazine, *Mark Friedman, Caterpillar's quality education supervisor, said the company wants "to fulfill the supplier partnership concept by assisting and supporting continuous improvement—to satisfy supplier's business needs and our own supplier certification program." The Institute provides suppliers with the training needed to improve. The earthmoving equipment giant requires that suppliers submit an annual quality improvement plan as part of the recertification process. The plan is supervised by a team from purchasing, quality, and manufacturing (led by purchasing) that has the power to recommend specific training if it finds a need. The first courses developed, on statistical process control, are still at the core of the Quality Institute curriculum.*

One lesson we hope we've been able to get across is that Supply Chain Management is a process that never ends. The goal is not to get through the steps in this book, then sit back and rest on your laurels. You can't do that because somewhere out there is a competitor who's busy figuring out how to do what you do faster or cheaper or with better quality—or all three! The only remedy is continuous improvement. And the only way you can continue to improve is if your suppliers continue to improve, too. That's what Supply Chain Management is all about.

The Supplier Continuous Value Improvement Process

When discussing a program for helping to keep your suppliers on track, we prefer the term "continuous **value** improvement process" (CVIP) instead of the more common "continuous improvement process" (CIP). Adding the word "value" helps keep the focus on the goal of improvement. Too often, companies get hung up on just hitting numerical targets. They forget that the real goal is to improve value and to eliminate anything that doesn't add value.

The good news is that once you've reached this point in your SCM process, many of the tools for continuous improvement are already in place. You're using supplier report cards and performance indexes to measure performance and diagnose problems. In many cases, the greatest barrier to improvement is your own inability to follow up on the assessments. If a report card shows delivery times slipping, do something about it—**now**! Don't wait until you've got a full-blown crisis. And follow up in a way that's appropriate for two companies that are committed to a long-term relationship.

Supplier Awareness Days

For CVIP to really take hold with your suppliers, however, you'll have to go beyond detecting problems and putting our fires. Instead, you've got to take an active role in helping your suppliers introduce new programs with substantial, long-term benefits. Many of the tools and processes for quality and continuous value improvement—electronic data interchange (EDI), statistical process control (SPC), set-up reduction programs, and so on—are outside the scope of this book. Your company probably already employs some of them. Or you may be in the process of adopting one of these programs at the behest of one of your own customers. If so, we urge you to pass along the benefits to your suppliers. Invite them to annual or semi-annual tutorials— Supplier Awareness Days—to introduce quality programs and explain how and why they work. You can choose from numerous topics for your Supplier Awareness Days. Here are a few:

- Electronic data interchange (EDI)
- Bar coding
- Performance indexes
- Cost of procurement program
- Corrective action program
- ISO 9000/QS 9000 program
- Statistical process control (SPC)
- Set-up reduction
- Value analysis program
- Total quality management program (TQM)

Finally, don't be close-minded to the fact that your suppliers may be using more advanced CVIP tools than your company. Chrysler, among other companies, was humble enough to recognize that it could learn much from its suppliers on the journey to quality.

Step 11 EXERCISE
CVIP in Your Supply Chain

Take this opportunity to see how your company compares to its suppliers on the tools of the Continuous Value Improvement Process. Put a check mark indicating which CVIP tools you and your suppliers use currently. This information will help you determine which suppliers can best benefit from a CVIP program sponsored by your company. In addition, you will find out which suppliers have the most to teach you.

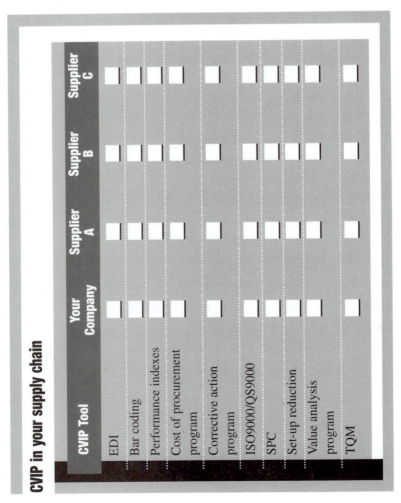

Figure 11-1. *Compare your suppliers on the tools of the CVIP.*

Measuring the Distance Traveled So Far

" You can't stand up and say, 'Next Tuesday, we're going to be different.' Because if people don't believe it, don't understand it, don't know why, it doesn't happen. *"*

Phil Condit,
CEO & Chairman, Boeing

You'll know your Supply Chain Management program is a success *when it's working for your suppliers, too. Boeing has some of the most rigorous supplier standards in any industry. The aerospace giant is continually reducing its number of suppliers and forging closer alliances with those that remain. Most of the company's parts are single-sourced. Generally, the only reason for two suppliers is if there's a concern about the performance of the primary supplier. In addition to its single-source philosophy, Boeing believes that establishing long-term relationships is the best way to manage costs. In the aerospace industry, this translates into customer-supplier relationships that last ten to thirty years. Although Boeing will terminate a company that can't meet performance standards, it prefers not to change suppliers. If a supplier falls short, Boeing will stand by the company as long as it shows a willingness to work hard towards a solution. No supplier would deny that Boeing is a demanding customer. However, the aerospace giant's attention makes the suppliers much better companies.*

Congratulations! If you've completed the steps to this point, your Supply Chain Management program is in place and running. Now, let's take a look back at where we've traveled so far. Your SCM program is never complete, of course. The global business climate simply doesn't allow it. However, you will reach significant milestones along the way. It's important to recognize them, to reflect on your accomplishments, and to gather your forces for the next phase. This chapter will help summarize what you've accomplished and will look at what lies ahead.

The Four Phases of Implementation

The activities involved in implementing Supply Chain Management can be separated into four stages or phases:

1. **Supplier Improvement Strategy**
2. **Supplier Assessment**
3. **Supplier Continuous Value Improvement Process**
4. **Supplier Acknowledgment**

Most of this book is concerned with the first two phases, which are the steps you go through in getting your SCM program up and running. (Some activities between the two phases overlap, which is why the lists that follow don't correspond exactly to the preceding steps.) Even when you get your program under way, you'll no doubt find that you have different supplier groups in different phases of the program at any one time. In one commodity family, for example, your SCM program might be well established with good suppliers in long-term relationships. Meanwhile, you might be just introducing SCM to the suppliers in another commodity group. Individual suppliers may be fully involved in the program while others may be lower on the learning curve.

If you find that you can check off most of the activities in Phases 1 and 2, you've traveled a long way. In fact, you may find that the greatest strides taken have been in your attitude toward your suppliers!

Phase 3, as we mentioned in Step 11, goes above and beyond the scope of this book. But if you've come this far, you are ready for Phase 4, which involves recognizing your suppliers for their accomplishments.

Phase 1: Supplier Improvement Strategy

Planting the seeds for success

In the first phase of your SCM program, your company made a commitment to Supply Chain Management and set its initial goals. A supply chain team was formed. The team began to formulate a strategy. Education was a key part of this early phase, as you, your team, and, to a certain degree, your whole company, learned about SCM. Remember, all the evidence (Figure 12-1) is strongly in favor of

Supply Chain Management benefits

Benefits to Your Company	Benefits to Your Suppliers
• Improved quality	• Improved quality
• Better price	• Reduced cost
• Continuous improvement	• Continuous improvement
• Improved communication	• Improved communication
• Inventory reduction	• Reduced cycle times
• On-time delivery	• Increased business
• No overages	• Improved payment terms
• No shortages	• Long-term commitment

Figure 12-1. *SCM is the proverbial "win-win" situation.*

Supply Chain Management. You also developed your SCM tools and began to apply them. By the time you complete all the activities in this phase, you're showing real results.

CHECKLIST FOR SUPPLY CHAIN MANAGEMENT, PHASE 1

Step 1: Commit to SCM as a Business Strategy

- ◯ Obtain management commitment and participation
- ◯ Retain an outside resource
- ◯ Set up a cost/benefit analysis
  - Necessary to sell SCM to your management and suppliers' management
- ◯ Educate the organization about the Supply Chain Management process
  - Why SCM is necessary
  - The goals of SCM
  - Department responsibilities under SCM

Step 2: Put the SCM Team Together

- ◯ Develop a cross-functional SCM team
- ◯ Educate the team about the SCM process

Step 3: Develop Goals and Objectives

- ◯ Formulate goals that match the company's business goals
- ◯ Begin to develop a detailed set of objectives

Step 4: Structure the Supply Chain

- ◯ Develop supplier selection tools
  - Commodity chart
  - Supplier selection criteria
- ◯ Select your first group of suppliers

Step 5: Develop Your Report Card Rating System

- ◯ Select the elements you want to measure
- ◯ Establish your measurement criteria

◯ Create and administer report cards

Step 7: Educate Your Suppliers

◯ Hold a Supplier Symposium

Step 8: Obtain 100% Agreement on Specifications

◯ Develop parts/materials specifications

◯ Achieve 100% agreement on specifications

Step 10: Evaluate Bids Using Supply Chain Performance Indexes

◯ Develop supplier rating indexes

◯ Perform ratings calculations

◯ Calculate performance indexes

Phase 2: Supplier Assessment

Assessing your suppliers is an ongoing process. Technically, there are assessments incorporated in all four phases of your SCM program. In fact, you could say that your whole SCM program is about assessing your suppliers and helping them improve. However, in Phase 2 we refer specifically to the tactical supply chain assessment. That's the process, initiated in Steps 6 and 9, for developing and administering a detailed assessment questionnaire. Eventually, you will have completed the assessment process with all your major suppliers. You'll have also performed an assessment before signing a major contract with a new supplier. The broad objectives of a supplier assessment are to:

- Assure that a supplier has adequate systems and process capabilities
- Eliminate the causes of quality and delivery problems

CHECKLIST FOR SUPPLY CHAIN MANAGEMENT, PHASE 2:

Step 6: Develop Your Tactical Supply Chain Assessment

◯ Develop a schedule for assessing your suppliers, beginning with the top 5%

◯ Design your supplier assessment questionnaire

☐ Form your cross-functional assessment team

The American Society for Quality (ASQ) recommends that an assessment team include the following representatives:

- Quality
- Purchasing
- Engineering
- Manufacturing

☐ Train your assessment team

- Review the assessment process
- Review assessment checklists
- Participate in assessment training
- Practice your assessment on a division of your own company

☐ Test your questionnaire

Step 9: Perform a Tactical Supply Chain Assessment

☐ Hold an introductory conference in the supplier's plant to explain why you are there

☐ Compare current performance with past performance

☐ Document both positive and negative information

☐ Maintain consistency of evaluation from assessment to assessment

☐ Hold a closing conference to present the assessment findings

☐ Communicate the findings in a final report

☐ Have the supplier develop a corrective action plan

Phase 3: Supplier Continuous Value Improvement Process

The activities noted in Phase 3, and discussed in Step 11, are the engine that will enable your SCM program to continue to reap benefits for your company and your suppliers. It will be one of the primary missions of your Supply Chain Management team as your program grows to maturity.

CHECKLIST FOR SUPPLY CHAIN MANAGEMENT, PHASE 3:

Step 11: Keep Suppliers On Track with CVIP (Continuous Value Improvement Process)

- Follow up supplier assessment
- Recommend supplier corrective action
- Initiate a continuous value improvement program
- Set objectives for your CVIP
    - Improve the supplier's quality performance
    - Improve the supplier's delivery performance
    - Improve specifications
    - Hold regular review meetings with suppliers to develop a corrective action plan
    - Correct the deficiencies uncovered in the supplier assessment
- Hold Supplier Awareness Days

Phase 4: Acknowledging Your Suppliers

It's important to recognize important milestones along your Supply Chain Management journey. Foremost among these is the success of your suppliers. When suppliers meet the goals of your SCM program, let them know it. Treat it as an honor when they:

- Achieve quality goals
- Achieve delivery goal
- Achieve total cost and service goals
- Pass the latest assessment goals
- Fully meet agreed-upon specifications

Many industry-leading companies hold an annual honors day or **supplier recognition ceremony** to award plaques to their best suppliers. It's a practice we endorse wholeheartedly. Award a plaque from your company that states the name of the supplier and the year they met SCM targets. The year is important. It underscores the fact that SCM is a continuous process and that awards must be earned annually. We also recommend that you present two plaques: one for the corporate offices and one for the plant. Present the plaque at the supplier's facility and try to have as many of the supplier's employees attend as possible. If you can present it on the shop floor, all the better.

Step 12 EXAMPLES
Supplier Recognition

Milliken & Company holds a supplier recognition ceremony every year. It takes advantage of the ceremony to address last year's performance, next year's focus, and next year's goals.

Honda of America annually presents awards for quality, delivery, production support, productivity improvement, best plant manager, and special awards. Here are a few of the annual results Honda celebrated at a supplier conference recognizing 70 companies:

- 28 suppliers had zero ppm defects
- 58 suppliers achieved quality goals
- 53 suppliers were very close to ppm goals

AT&T Switching and Transmission Systems holds a yearly Partners in Excellence" conference. Honorees are selected by a cross-functional commodity team. At the conference, suppliers tell what they did to achieve the award.

Taking Supply Chain Management to the Next Level

*"*A woman rushed up to a famous pianist after a concert and cried, 'I'd give my life to play as beautifully as you do.' The pianist replied, 'I did.'*"*

When Xerox adopted Supply Chain Management principles *in 1980, the company's signature copy machines exhibited less than stellar performance. They seemed to be down more than they were operational and the Xerox repair technician was an all-too-familiar sight at offices everywhere. The company had serious image problems and it needed to take drastic measures.*

Fast-forward to the 1990s: Xerox is transformed. Its copy machines and other products are once again in the vanguard thanks to the successful supplier partnerships the company has forged over time.

The numbers behind Xerox's return to form are impressive and illustrate the importance of committing to an SCM program for the long term. Applying SCM concepts, the company reduced its number of suppliers from a bloated 5000 to a lean 400, a staggering 92% drop, between 1980 and 1993. For ten consecutive years, Xerox reduced its product costs by 10% per year, reduced its material costs by 12% per year, and slashed its inbound logistics by 13% per year. Over a ten-year period, the company cut its overall design costs by 33% and its prototype costs by 50%.

Firmly committed to supplier training, Xerox spends $500,000 annually on *programs such as Just-In-Time Manufacturing, Activity-Based Costing, Employee Empowerment, and Total Quality Management. The return on investment goes beyond the bottom line. By freely sharing information, promoting SCM practices, and placing a premium on performance, Xerox inspires its suppliers to jump on the supply chain bandwagon. Success breeds success.*

Supply Chain Management, we are fond of pointing out, is a quality journey. But, in our analogy, it is not the kind of journey that has a particular destination and abruptly ends. Like the mythical Oz, you can't easily find all the secrets to success in the Emerald City. As the man behind the curtain might tell you, you have had the power to effect change all along. The secret is to stick with the program. The goal is *continuous* quality improvement. It's a moving target. SCM is a never-ending journey.

That does not mean success will always be out of reach. Your company will experience a constant stream of success along the way. But the journey must continue.

There will be short-term benefits. By reducing the number of suppliers, issuing report cards, and adopting other SCM principles, you will immediately see results. But truly spectacular results await those patient companies that follow the Supply Chain Management path for three years, five years, ten years, and beyond. It will take vision, commitment, and belief. But you will not have to travel down the SCM path on a wing and a prayer. As you will see at the end of this chapter, you can follow the lead of pioneers whose impressive successes will blaze your trail. Using them as your guide, take the long view and stay focused on your organization's SCM journey.

Articulate Your Vision

Supplier-Directed

Explain your long-term goals and share them with your suppliers. That way both your company and its suppliers will have yardsticks by which to measure success. Include your suppliers in the equation. Let them know up front what you will expect from them and show them your commitment over the long haul.

As Figure 13-1 shows, prepare a chart that puts in writing your yearly goals across a spectrum of performance areas. Of course, you will want to revisit these goals at least annually and adjust them according to actual results. By breaking down "excellence" into a number of discrete categories, you will be giving your suppliers multiple targets and showing them the well-rounded profile you desire.

The five-year target goals listed in Figure 13-1 represent huge improvements in performance. By reducing manufacturing throughput time from four weeks to 24 hours, a supplier would be making a 96% improvement. With a one-week part lead-time, instead of ten weeks, a supplier would offer a 90% improvement. Instead of meeting a requested delivery date about three out of every four times, the eventual goal is 100% compliance. Keep in mind that we are talking about a five-year period; nobody expects overnight miracles. But you should expect steady progress.

As you measure excellence on a supplier-by-supplier basis, you will also want to keep an overview of your entire supplier base. The goal is to reduce the quantity of suppliers while you simultaneously improve their overall quality. You can track the trend and confirm that it is moving in a positive direction. Periodically, gather internal data and poll your suppliers to determine the percentage of your supplier base that meets the following criteria:

- Maintains performance levels
- Meets quality goals

Sample five-year vision targets for suppliers

Category	Current	1-Year Goal	2-Year Goal	3-Year Goal	4-Year Goal	5-Year Goal
Manufacturing through-put time	4 weeks	2 weeks	1 week	3 days	1 1/2 days	1 day
Delivery to customer needed date	76%	88%	95%	97%	98%	100%
New product introduction time	24 months	12 months	9 months	8 months	7 months	6 months
Supplier lead time	10 weeks	7 weeks	5 weeks	3 weeks	2 weeks	1 week
Cost of quality	12%	10%	9%	7%	6%	5%
Equipment availability	60%	70%	75%	80%	85%	90%

Figure 13-1. *Measuring supplier excellence.*

- Meets continuous value improvement performance (CVIP) goals
- Reduces lead times
- Is involved in design
- Uses statistical process control (SPC)

Compare the "new" supplier measurements we just listed with more traditional measurements:

- Number purchase orders per buyer
- Number line items per buyer
- Dollars committed per buyer
- Average open dollar commitment
- Time to process purchase order document
- Number line items past due
- Cost per purchase order

These values measure attributes of volume and efficiency. They do have a place in your organization's recordkeeping. The traditional measurements offer a basic comparative analysis of your suppliers. But they do not take competitive business success into account. To keep your eye on the bigger prize, you will want to maintain a log of the new SCM supplier measurements.

While we are challenging traditional beliefs, let's revisit some points made earlier regarding the characteristics you should be looking for in your suppliers. Let go of the outdated win-or-lose price-based paradigm. Instead, focus on suppliers who know what their customers want and provide excellent customer service. Choose suppliers who are ready to become an extension of your business. Look for suppliers who create platforms for continuous improvement. And turn to suppliers who are prepared for constant change. After all, change is really the only thing of which we can be sure. You will want suppliers who are able to go along with you for the ride.

Internally Directed

You will also want to establish internal long-term goals for your company. Considering the improved performances your suppliers will offer and the systemic changes your company will be making, you can expect significant benefits over time. Figure 13-2 lists goals that can tie directly to your company's bottom line. The numbers may appear excessively optimistic. Remember, however, that we are looking at a five-year period of intense effort.

The target goals in Figure 13-2 are all cash-related benefits. They could be viewed from different vantage points, however. The reduction in inventory and space requirements, for example, could free up space that your company might use to expand manufacturing capabilities.

Five-year internal targets

Category	5-Year Goal
Reduce purchased costs	10 to 20%
Reduce space requirements	30 to 50%
Reduce inventory levels	30 to 90%
Reduce total product cycle time	40 to 60%
Reduce supplier lead times	25 to 35%
Reduce price of non-conformance	30 to 50%
Reduce rework	20 to 30%
Reduce scrap	10 to 20%
Reduce work-in-process	25 to 35%

Figure 13-2. *Cash-related benefits.*

We include some of the reduction targets in Figure 13-2 in the following summarized Supply Chain Management goals. As your program matures, you can whittle down the internal management results you will be looking for, on a year-to-year basis, to four general categories:

1. Cost reductions
2. Quality improvements
3. Reduction in total product cycle time
4. Improvement in responsiveness to customer wants

It's easy to become lost in the details. When you look past the daily logistics of your SCM program and can see the forest for the trees, these four categories comprise the desired underlying improvements. If you are making significant progress in each of the aforementioned areas over time, you are well on your way to SCM success.

The Power of Zeal

The difference between a Supply Chain Management program that works and one that falls apart can often be traced to one "secret" ingredient: zeal. In these overly-cynical, "Dilbert-ized" times, it's easy to dismiss any new program as so much corporate blather. It's hard to move away from comfort levels. It's hard to change an entrenched culture. Those who choose to go to the front of the pack and lead by example run the risk of being challenged, scorned, and chastised. But those companies that choose to ignore innovation and stick with traditional approaches run the risk of losing market share and being left in the dust.

That brings us back to "gospel spreading," one of the primary duties of the SCM team that we outlined early in the book. It's not enough to merely spread the word. You have to spread the word with enthusiasm. You have to walk the talk. You have to express a passion for Supply Chain Management and make believers out of cynics.

You can tweak the numbers and fine-tune the details but zeal is the one item that must remain consistent. Zeal will carry your SCM program through the years so that your company can post impressive long-term performance gains. Zeal will help you stay the course with your suppliers and your co-workers. Best of all, zeal is free!

Be a risk-taker. Let your enthusiasm shine through. The success of your SCM program depends on it. Though it may not be fashionable—and is sometimes difficult—the rewards are tremendous.

And so we end our book where we began with a final bit of encouragement from Dr. Deming, the guru of quality management, from one of his landmark speeches: *You don't have to do this... Survival is not compulsory.*

Step 13 EXERCISE
Take the Long View

Using Figure 13-3, determine a three-year goal for each of the performance items. Make a note in your tickler file to return to this exercise three years from the date you first begin your SCM program and compare your actual results.

Three-year check-up

Performance Item	Typical 3-Year Target	Your 3-Year Goal	Your 3-Year Actual
Total cycle time reduction (order to shipment)	50%		
Total inventory decrease	50%		
Percentage of your sales orders that reach customers on time	98%		
Reduction of supplier base	50%		
Average supplier lead time reduction	50%		
Reduction of scrap, rework, and warranty costs	50%		
Decrease of your cost to produce	20%		
Reduction of overall cost of quality	50%		
Decrease of direct material costs	10%		
Reduce product development cycle time	50%		

Figure 13-3. *Supply Chain Management reengineering targets, goals, and results.*

Success Stories

When you become discouraged during your quality journey—and you will—return to these inspiring examples. They are real companies that produced real results. Of course, they also shed some real blood, sweat, and tears along the way. Let them serve as guideposts to help keep you on the path.

Chrysler

The country's number three auto maker has had its share of problems, including its infamous federal bailout. In 1989, Robert Lutz, Chrysler's president, gathered the company's top 25 suppliers and told them, "All I want is your brainpower, not your margins." That was a fairly revolutionary statement coming from an industry that typically beats its suppliers up over price. But that was only the beginning. Through alliances established with its key suppliers, Chrysler asked its new "partners" to help the car manufacturer in three areas:

1. Focus on what Chrysler was doing wrong. (Previously, this was

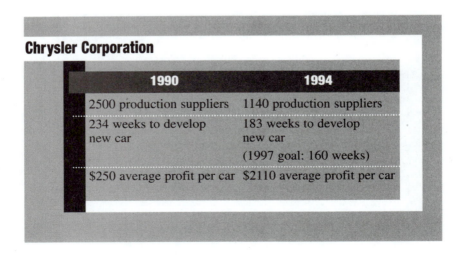

Chrysler Corporation

1990	1994
2500 production suppliers	1140 production suppliers
234 weeks to develop new car	183 weeks to develop new car (1997 goal: 160 weeks)
$250 average profit per car	$2110 average profit per car

Figure 13-4. *Sample SCM improvements at Chrysler.*

a taboo subject between customers and suppliers.)

2. Make suggestions that involved materials and parts from lower-tier suppliers. (If this advice was solicited at all, it would follow item number three.)

3. Focus on what key suppliers were doing wrong.

In this way, Chrysler made its suppliers partners in bringing down costs and the selling prices of cars. The results have been striking.

Using supplier partnerships, Chrysler saved $500 million in production costs on the 1994 Neon. The company's suppliers managed 68% of the total production costs. Compared to comparable models, Chrysler used 33% fewer engineers to design the Neon. In 1995, the company estimated it was able to reduce its production costs 20% to 40% by working together with its suppliers.

Chrysler's 1997 U.S. market share, 14.7%, is its highest in 25 years. Since 1992, it has posted the highest return on assets among American auto makers. Not bad for a company that was once on the verge of bankruptcy!

A.W. Chesterton Company

Small and mid-size companies have success stories to tell as well. This

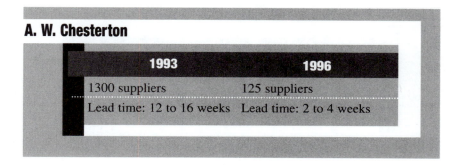

Figure 13-5. *Sample SCM improvements at A. W. Chesterton.*

Stoneham, Massachusetts manufacturer of seals, pumps, and packing generates $200 million in yearly sales. Chesterton expects its suppliers, which must be among the top three for their commodity groups in quality, service, and price, to participate in design.

Motorola

Marketplace success for communications giant Motorola depends on developing relationships with component suppliers that meet the following criteria:

- Keep pace in attaining perfect quality
- Stay on the leading edge of technology
- Practice Just-In-Time manufacturing
- Offer cost-competitive service

Motorola aggressively trains its suppliers and requires them to analyze how quality defects add to their own costs. Bruce Bendhoff, president of Craftsman Custom Metal Fabricators, says, "Doing a pretty good job is never satisfactory for Motorola. They always want to know why a supplier is not doing better....Pricing is a tough nut. But no matter how tough the negotiation is, you always know that you are going to get together. We sit, we talk, we reason, and we conclude."

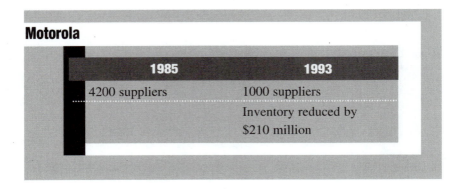

Figure 13-6. *Sample SCM improvements at Motorola.*

NCR-Workstation Products Division

NCR turned its supplier paradigm around and now places its top priority on quality, followed by delivery, then price. Its suppliers are actively involved in the design phase.

Harley-Davidson

Despite a long and proud tradition, Harley's overseas competitors badly clobbered the legendary motorcycle manufacturer in the 1970s. The company nearly crumbled. Today, the pride is back and Harley could be a "poster" company for Supply Chain Management. Its suppliers must perform JIT techniques, including statistical process control, continuous improvement, and employee involvement.

NCR

Base Year	3-to-5 Year Results
2000+ suppliers	150 suppliers
12 to 18-month product development time	6-month product development time
Contracts renegotiated yearly	"Evergreen" contracts
Spotty parts quality	50 to 100 PPM on incoming parts
	70% reduction of parts shortages
	50% reduction in inventory

Figure 13-7. *Sample SCM improvements at NCR's Workstation Products Division.*

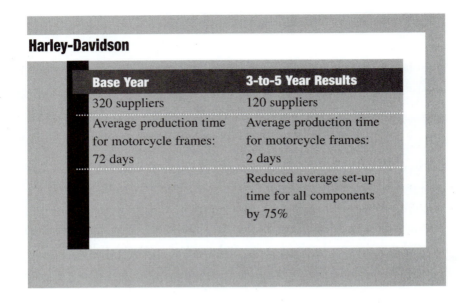

Figure 13-8. *Sample SCM improvements at Harley-Davidson.*

QUESTIONS? COMMENTS? FEEDBACK?

We invite your inquiries about any of the material covered in this book. As a forum for professionals interested in SCM, we rely on your feedback to help shape future editions.

SHARE YOUR SUCCESS!

We are especially interested in your SCM success stories. Let us know how you are doing. Perhaps we will feature your company in future editions.

Direct all correspondence to:
   Chip Long and Dr. Gay Meyer
   Sacred Cow Stories
   World Class Consulting Group
   P.O. Box 2722
   Seal Beach, CA 90740

FAX: (562) 598-4885